Project Communication
from Start to Finish

Project Communication from Start to Finish

The Dynamics of Organizational Success

Geraldine E. Hynes

BEP BUSINESS EXPERT PRESS

Project Communication from Start to Finish: The Dynamics of Organizational Success

First published in 2019 by
Business Expert Press, LLC
222 East 46th Street, New York, NY 10017
www.businessexpertpress.com

ISBN-13: 978-1-94999-154-3 (paperback)
ISBN-13: 978-1-94999-155-0 (e-book)

Business Expert Press Portfolio and Project Management Collection

Collection ISSN: 2156-8189 (print)
Collection ISSN: 2156-8200 (electronic)

Cover and interior design by Exeter Premedia Services Private Ltd., Chennai, India

First edition: 2019

10 9 8 7 6 5 4 3 2 1

Printed in the United States of America.

Abstract

Skills in project management are critical in a broad range of businesses and industries. A key knowledge area for project managers is communication. In fact, research shows that 90 percent of a project manager's time is spent communicating with various stakeholders. This book offers techniques and strategies that enhance communication in diverse environments. It offers innovative ways to bridge cultural gaps, increase understanding, and ensure project success. Project managers will learn how to build trust and rapport, manage conflict, listen, communicate expectations, give performance feedback, and overcome communication barriers. A look to the future includes best practices for using emerging technology when communicating with distributed teams. The Project Management Institute's standards for ethical and professional conduct are emphasized as they apply to managerial communication behaviors throughout the project life cycle. This book's concise format makes it a readable, practical guide, and it can also be used as a reference for fixing the most frequent communication breakdowns. Cases and examples are presented to illustrate applications of the communication principles from a project's start to finish.

Keywords

project communication; managerial communication; interpersonal communication; project management; project leadership; project teams; project success; diversity; cultural competence; trust

Abstract

Contents

Acknowledgments

I am grateful to my BEP team for making this book a reality. Sheri Dean originated the idea and convinced me it would be a valued addition to the Project Management literature. Tim Kloppenborg and Scott Isenberg, both of whom are exemplary project managers, were instrumental in shaping the content and structure. Charlene Kronstedt oversaw the production with her customary patience and skill.

Some material in this book was drawn from *Get Along, Get It Done, Get Ahead: Interpersonal Communication in the Diverse Workplace*, my first book for BEP, with the publisher's permission.

I salute Pam Zelbst, PhD, PMP, author, Professor of Supply Chain Management and Director of the Center for Innovation & Technology at Sam Houston State University, for generously sharing her time, wisdom, and encouragement over the years, and for reviewing the manuscript.

Vic Sower, PhD, CQE, author, Quality Management Consultant at Sower & Associates, LLC, and Distinguished Professor Emeritus of Management, Sam Houston State University, also took time to review the manuscript. A true mentor, he cheered me on throughout the composing process and provided thoughtful suggestions, particularly in Chapter 5.

I am also indebted to Mike Power, SHSU Online instructional designer, who worked his magic on the book's graphics, helping me create clear and simple illustrations of key concepts.

Finally, I am most grateful to Jim Hynes because he is always at my side and on my side.

CHAPTER 1

Introduction to Project Communication

Chapter Objectives

This chapter provides a rationale for the book and sets the stage for its content. It begins by explaining that communication is a key knowledge area for project managers and presents research findings that show the correlation between communication effectiveness and project success as well as organizational success. Next, the chapter introduces the *Guide to the Project Management Body of Knowledge (PMBOK® Guide)*, the premier resource for project managers. The chapter highlights sections of the *Guide* that focus on communication competencies for project managers.

In the third section of this chapter, project life cycles are described, as well as the role of communication at each stage of the life cycle. Finally, the chapter provides an overview of the conceptual model at the heart of this book—"The Sequence for Success"—and shows how the model embodies critical ideas about project communication that are found in the *PMBOK® Guide*.

Communication as a Key Knowledge Area for Project Managers

Communication competence is important for today's project managers. The importance is increasing, for several reasons. For one thing, organizations are becoming more complex, and managers' responsibilities are growing. Overall, the role of the project manager has evolved over the past 50 years from being the administrator of a project toward a much more managerial and leadership position, fulfilling an organizational strategic need.

A second influence on the importance of effective communication is the competition inherent in a global environment, with accompanying demands for speed, quality, and service. A third factor is the diversity of the contemporary workplace, which often extends beyond geographical boundaries. Fourth, advances in telecommunications have developed, adding new expectations for managerial communication regarding speed and accuracy. In short, project managers must have the ability to communicate to a diverse group of stakeholders in a rapidly changing global context.

> The importance of managerial communication is evolving.

Communication and Project Managers' Success

The project manager's role is one of the most challenging jobs in any organization, because it requires a broad understanding of the various areas that must be coordinated and requires strong interpersonal skills. It is widely acknowledged that the final outcome of the project depends mainly on the project manager.

To determine what capabilities and competencies are most important for a project manager's success, a content analysis was conducted of 762 job advertisements for project managers across a range of industries and countries. The results are shown in Table 1.1.

Table 1.1 Recruiters' top requirements for project managers

Competency	Advertisement (%)
Communication	61.7
Technical skills	43.5
Stakeholder management	41.7
Cost management	37.4
Time management	32.7
Education	28.6
Planning	26.1
Leadership	24.4
Team building and management	22.6
Certification	20.5

As Table 1.1 shows, the top competency that recruiters sought was communication (61.7 percent).[1]

Martha Buelt and Connie Plowman, prominent coaches and educators in project management, also identify communication as a key strength for project managers. They describe this strength as:

> You speak and write clearly. You place high value on human interaction, talking with—not to—people. You tell stories to enliven your ideas, gain commitment, and maintain enthusiasm. You ask good questions, listen well, and help others express their feelings. You "think out loud" and encourage collaboration.[2]

Drilling down to specific behaviors, Buelt and Plowman define a "strength" as the ability to do something consistently well. Communication is a strength for project managers if they communicate consistently well what stakeholders need to know. Components of project managers' communication competency are summarized in Table 1.2.

Jennifer Jones, director of the training firm AMA Enterprise, affirms that communication competency is essential for managerial success:

> Communication is actually an umbrella term for such core skills as listening, thinking clearly, interpreting organizational concepts, being alert to non-verbal signals as well as dealing with any stress or emotional issues in working with co-workers or supervisors. Indeed, understood correctly communications helps a person understand a situation, resolve differences and build trust.[3]

Table 1.2 Project managers' communication strengths

Building blocks	Behavior
Skill	Active listening
Talent	Asks questions. Interested in others' thoughts
Knowledge	Knows that words matter
Experiences	Talks with people, not at people
PM tools and techniques	Effectively uses the project communication plan
PM core competencies	Clearly communicates in oral and written formats

Jones concludes that it is essential for project managers to encourage collaboration because collaboration leads to better solutions, a productive workplace, and achievement of business objectives.

Communication and Organizational Success

Effective communication not only improves project managers' performance, it improves organizational success. Towers Watson, a company that provides management consulting services, conducted research on 651 organizations from a broad range of industries and regions over a 10-year period. They found that those companies that communicate effectively are 350 percent more likely to significantly outperform their industry peers than those companies that do not communicate effectively. Other key findings focused on manager communication:

- Managers at the best companies are three times more likely to communicate clearly to their employees the behaviors that are expected of them, instead of being focused on cost.
- Managers at the best companies pay careful attention to their employees in their change planning; they communicate reasons for changes, provide training, and support the employees, instead of using a top-down approach. Extensive managerial communication improves the likelihood of successful change.
- Managers at the best companies are more than twice as likely to use new social media technologies to facilitate collaboration on work projects. Furthermore, they typically see better employee productivity and financial performance.[4]

Here is even more compelling evidence of the importance of effective communication for organizational success. The Project Management Institute (PMI) published an in-depth report, *Pulse of the Profession: The High Cost of Low Performance: The Essential Role of Communications*. The report was the result of research conducted among over 1,000 project managers and executives involved in large capital projects (at least US $250,000) worldwide. PMI's study provides evidence that for every

US $1 billion spent on a project, a startling 56 percent is at risk due to ineffective communication with stakeholders. Undoubtedly, effective communication is the most crucial success factor in a complex and competitive business climate.[5]

> Organizations cannot afford to overlook communication because it is a key element of project success and long-term profitability.

The PMBOK® Guide

The Project Management Institute, Inc., (PMI) is the premier association for professionals who are involved with project teams. PMI is a global nonprofit organization serving more than 2.9 million professionals including over 540,000 members in 208 countries and territories around the world. As of 2018 there are 300 chapters and 10,000 volunteers serving local members in over 80 countries.

One of PMI's major functions is to create industry standards, such as those in *A Guide to the Project Management Body of Knowledge (PMBOK®)*, which has been recognized by the American National Standards Institute (ANSI). The Sixth Edition of the *PMBOK® Guide*, published in 2017, is the most recent. Other PMI services include research, education, publication, networking-opportunities in local chapters, hosting conferences and training seminars, and providing accreditation in project management.

Knowledge Areas

The *PMBOK® Guide* identifies ten knowledge areas that are critical for project management success (Section 1.2.4.5). They are:

1. Project integration management
2. Project scope management
3. Project schedule management
4. Project cost management
5. Project quality management
6. Project resource management

7. Project communications management
8. Project risk management
9. Project procurement management
10. Project stakeholder management

Although these knowledge areas are interrelated, they are defined separately from the project management perspective. In addition, PMI recognizes that some projects may require other knowledge areas, although these ten are the most frequently relevant to projects.

Communication as a Knowledge Area

The *PMBOK® Guide* describes how each knowledge area is applied at each stage of the project life cycle. The seventh knowledge area in the preceding list, "Project Communications Management," is seen to be useful for planning, executing, monitoring and controlling processes (Sections 10.1–10.3). Communication is defined as "the exchange of information, intended or involuntary, between individuals and/or groups. The information exchanged can be in the form of ideas, instructions, or emotions" (Sections 10.1 and X4.7). The mechanisms by which information is exchanged can be:

- Written or oral
- Formal or informal
- Verbal or nonverbal
- Through technological media or face to face
- Internal or external
- Vertical or horizontal
- Official or unofficial

PMI recognizes that project managers spend most of their time communicating with their team and other stakeholders. "Effective communication builds a bridge between diverse stakeholders who may have different cultural and organizational backgrounds as well as different levels of expertise, perspectives, and interests." Further, a project's communications are seen as supported by efforts to prevent misunderstanding and miscommunication and by careful selection of the methods, messengers, and messages developed from the planning process.[6]

> Communication develops the relationships necessary for successful project and program outcomes.

According to the *PMBOK® Guide*, the fundamental attributes of effective communication activities are:

- Clarity on the purpose of the communication
- Understanding as much as possible about the receiver of the communications and tailoring the message to them
- Monitoring and measuring the effectiveness of the communications

In short, all communication should be clear and concise (Sections 10, X4.7). These attributes specified in the *Guide* are at the heart of communication theory and are undisputed.

Communication as a Leadership Skill

The *PMBOK® Guide* includes a section on leadership; the section identifies communication as a key skill and knowledge area for leaders who guide, motivate, and direct a team and who help an organization achieve its goals. The *Guide* lists 13 qualities and skills of a leader (Section 3.4.4.2). More than half of these qualities and skills are communication-based. They are:

1. Sharing the project's vision with all stakeholders
2. Being collaborative
3. Managing relationships and conflict by:
   a. Building trust
   b. Satisfying concerns
   c. Seeking consensus

    d. Applying persuasion, negotiation, compromise, and conflict resolution skills

    e. Developing and nurturing networks

4. Communicating by:

    a. Spending about 90 percent of their time on a project in communicating

    b. Managing expectations

    c. Accepting feedback graciously

    d. Giving feedback constructively

    e. Asking and listening

5. Being respectful, courteous, friendly, and ethical

6. Being culturally sensitive

7. Giving credit to others where due

> Project managers spend about 90 percent of their time communicating.

Communication Tools and Techniques

The *PMBOK® Guide* specifies a number of tools and techniques for enhancing communication when managing a project. The tools and techniques have application at various stages of a project's life cycle. They include oral and written, formal and informal methods and are summarized in Table 1.3.[7]

Table 1.3 PMBOK® Guide's communication tools and techniques

Purpose	Tool/technique
Data representation	*Stakeholder engagement* assessment matrix
Communication	Communication competence *Feedback* *Nonverbal* Presentations
Interpersonal and team skills	*Active listening* Communication styles assessment *Conflict management* *Cultural awareness* Meeting management

	Networking
	Observation/conversation
	Political awareness
Ungrouped tools and techniques	*Communication methods*
	Communication models
	Communication requirements analysis
	Communication technology
	Expert judgment
	Meetings
	Project management information system

As you review the *PMBOK® Guide*'s list of tools and techniques in Table 1.3, you can see how well they map to the topics directly addressed in this book. The techniques identified in the *Guide* that are also presented in this book are italicized in Table 1.3. It is safe to conclude that the PMI, sponsor of the *PMBOK® Guide*, is in accord with scholarly researchers and business professionals in that PMI recognizes similar skills and competencies as being essential for inclusion in a project manager's communication tool kit. References to *The PMBOK® Guide—Sixth Edition* are found throughout this book.

The Role of Communication in a Project's Life Cycle

According to the *PMBOK® Guide,* communications flow to project team members and other stakeholders throughout the project life cycle. A project life cycle is the series of phases that a project passes through from start to finish; it is the basic framework for managing the project. The phases may be sequential, iterative, or overlapping. Chapter 2 describes different types of project life cycles and their management methods in more detail.

Communication is critical at every stage of a project's life cycle. Effective communication ensures timely and appropriate planning, collection, creation, distribution, storage, retrieval, management, control, monitoring, and ultimate disposition of project information.[8]

If the previous paragraphs sound overwhelming and abstract, let's turn to Joseph Phillips, author of five books about project management, for a concrete example that you might more easily relate to. In a recent article he describes the following scenario:

Your favorite project team member enters your office. He says, "Hi. Got a real problem I could use some help with. I'm having a tough time understanding the project requirements on this deliverable." And you hear, "Blah, blah, blah, problem, blah, blah, tough, blah." It's not that you don't mean to understand your team member, it's just that you're not listening. You've got a bazillion things racing through your head; you're juggling seven different projects.

If only projects were as easy as, I communicated something to you and you did what I asked. Sometimes you, the project manager, have to do a lot of begging and pleading. You often know what needs to be done and you need to transfer that knowledge to your project team members, along with motivation, so they will go do it. And when you don't know what needs to be done, you expect your sub-project managers or team members to figure out approaches and solutions, sort out the details, and report the results back to you.

Phillips explains that communication is tough but easier when the project manager plans to communicate. Communication planning comes down to this key question: Who needs what information, when do they need it, and in what modality?

Who

Not all stakeholders need the same information. For instance, functional managers need to know information related to their employees on your project, such as schedules and time accountability. The project sponsor and key stakeholders need information on the project status, finances, and any variances in cost and time.

When

Depending on the stakeholders, information needs vary between daily, weekly, monthly, and "based on conditions in the project." For example, your project sponsor may ask for weekly status reports, but the project champion may ask for status reports just once a month. The secret is to schedule and, if possible, automate the communication demands as much as possible. Using your project management information system you can create macros, templates, even auto-generate reports on a regular schedule.

How

The best practice is to give stakeholders the information they need in the modality they'll be expecting. Some prefer a quick e-mail. Others require an extensive spreadsheet, report, and executive summaries. Some communication is expected in quick, ad-hoc meetings, while other messages may be best transmitted as a formal presentation accompanied by a PowerPoint slideshow.

> The project manager must be at the center of communications.

Philips concludes that, to be effective, project managers must listen to what's coming at them, what's being discussed among their project team, and what they're telling the stakeholders at every phase of the project life cycle. "You, the project manager, must be at the center of communications; you have to be the communications hub."[9]

Overview of the Sequence for Success Model

The conceptual model that is at the heart of this book is called the Sequence for Success. It consists of five levels, each one building atop the previous one, with the pinnacle representing productivity, project success, and organizational success. The following section of this chapter explain what's involved at each of the five levels and why it is located where it is in the model.

Level 1—Cornerstones

The Sequence for Success model has two cornerstones at its base level. The first cornerstone is *diversity appreciation*; the workforce is becoming increasingly diverse, and diversity is a competitive advantage for project teams and their sponsoring organizations.

Figure 1.1 Cornerstones of the sequence for success model

The second cornerstone is *cultural competence;* differences in team members' cultural values, customs, and communication patterns require project managers to be skillful in navigating among these differences. Culturally competent project managers know how to develop positive relationships with diverse team members that will positively impact members' loyalty, satisfaction, and productivity.

Let us now build on these cornerstones (Figure 1.1) to create a framework for the rest of the book. After reading this chapter, you will see how project managers who appreciate diversity and who have cultural competence are more likely to experience project success.

Levels 2 and 3—Interpersonal Communication and Work Relationships

Getting along with peers, team members, bosses, sponsors, and other stakeholders is mostly a matter of communication. To build strong relationships with all these constituencies you must interact with them

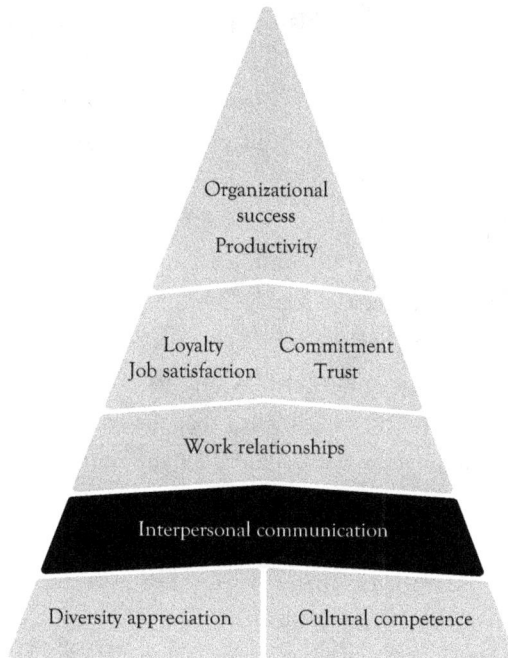

Figure 1.2 Communication and the sequence for success

regularly. As you will read, there can be no relationship if there is no communication. Therefore, communication and work relationships are the
next building blocks for project success. We will set these building blocks
on top of the two cornerstones already in place (Figure 1.2).

Let's think a little more about the impact of your interpersonal communication. If you're a project manager, your daily interactions with your
team typically centers on these ten topics, right?

1. Procedures
2. Guidance
3. Policies
4. Work conditions
5. Work problems
6. Solutions to work problems
7. Deadlines, goals
8. Corrective feedback
9. Positive feedback
10. Raises, promotions, and advancement

You might want to add to this list of topics, depending on your own unique project, but these are the top ten things that managers talk about on the job. You already know that your communication style when interacting with your team about these topics will significantly determine how well they do their jobs. Their performance depends on the clarity, accuracy, and timeliness of your instructions, information, and feedback.

But did you know that your communication style will also determine what they think about you as a team leader? An interesting study of 363 adults with an average of eight years of work experience focused on what they considered to be a "good boss." Contrary to what you might predict, the researchers found no evidence that the workers evaluated their bosses according to how the bosses used their authority, control, or power. Instead, the most important factor for judging their bosses to be good or bad was the extent to which the bosses showed appreciation, respect, or high regard for the workers. This factor is called "affiliation." By the way, sex did not seem to influence the workers' ratings of the quality of their leaders. Both male and female workers rated both male and female leaders as "good" bosses if their communication was high on affiliation.[10]

> Good project leaders show appreciation, respect, or high regard for the workers.

Making an effort to develop relationships with your project team will make your job easier. Ever wonder why your people don't comply with your demands/requests? After all, you are the leader. Here's why: your job title may give you authority, also known as position power, but if you want to influence your team, you also need personal power. Personal power derives from your credibility. The elements of managerial credibility are:

- Rank—position in the hierarchy
- Expertise—skill or knowledge
- Image—personal attractiveness
- Common ground—shared value
- Goodwill—personal relationships

It's that last item on the bulleted list that we're talking about here. Goodwill is how you get your people to put up with poor working conditions, long hours, stressful deadlines, and ambiguity. Goodwill is a product of personal relationships.

Position power = authority
Personal power = credibility

Level 4—Key Emotional Conditions

Let's add another building block to our Sequence for Success model, one that captures key emotional conditions caused by strong relationships. "Wait. Why should I worry about emotions and relationships with my team?" you may ask. "I have to work with these people, but I don't have to like them." True. In fact, if you ever find team members that you like well enough to become friends outside of work, that's a bonus. More often, however, the people we consider to be friends will disappear from our lives when they (or we) leave the organization.

On the other hand, a strong case can be made for trying to develop positive relationships with your team, so that certain emotional conditions occur. Among these key emotions are loyalty, satisfaction, commitment, and trust, represented by the new building block in Figure 1.3. Notice that "liking" is not on this list of emotions. You can trust people without liking them. You can also feel loyal, satisfied, and committed to a project without liking the actual work.

Project commitment means that your people will:

- Identify with the project's goals and values
- Want to belong to the project team
- Be willing to display effort on behalf of the project and team

Research consistently shows that low commitment leads to absenteeism, turnover, and unrest. On the other hand, high commitment leads to trust, quality and quantity of communication, involvement, and productivity.[11] So if you treat your team well, they will work harder to ensure the success of the project.

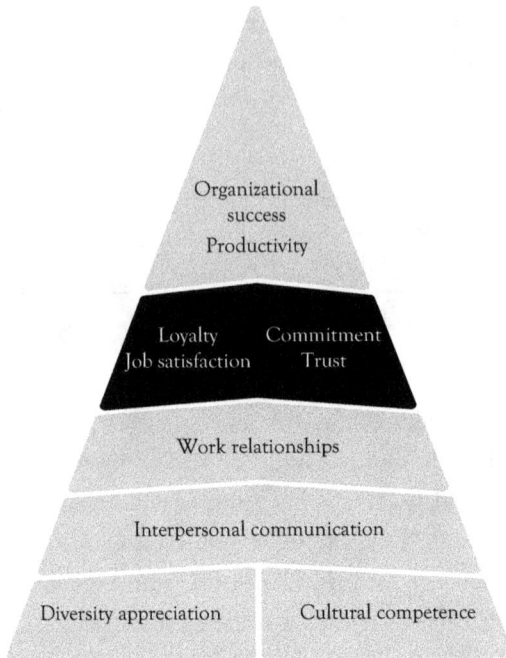

Figure 1.3 Key emotional conditions and the sequence for success

Level 5—Productivity and Performance Success

Let's finish building the Sequence for Success model by adding another block that represents productivity and success. The connection between job performance and key emotional conditions is well established. Figure 1.4 illustrates that when team members feel a sense of loyalty, commitment, job satisfaction, and trust, their productivity improves and, ultimately, the project and sponsoring organization will succeed.

Want more evidence for the truth of this Success model—that communication and commitment ultimately lead to success? In 2013, the PMI published results of their survey of 1,093 project managers, executives, and business owners who were involved in large capital projects worldwide. The business leaders agreed that *the most crucial success factor in project management is effective communication* to all stakeholders. Further, the study showed that highly effective communicators are *five times* more likely to be high performers than poor communicators, as measured by whether they finished the project on time, within budget, and according to the original goals.[12]

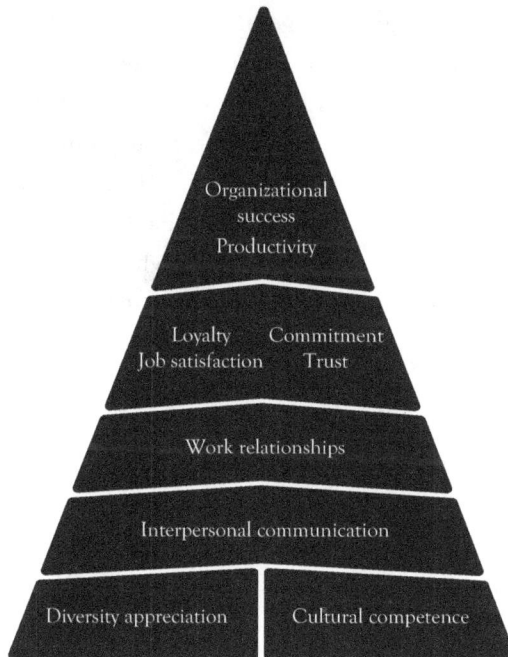

Figure 1.4 The complete sequence for success model

If you're still not convinced that project managers' communication leads to project success, here's even more evidence. In a 2012 review of 263 research studies across 192 companies, Gallup found that companies in the top quartile for "engaged" employees, compared with the bottom quartile, had 22 percent higher profitability, 10 percent higher customer ratings, 28 percent less theft, and 48 percent fewer safety incidents.[13]

Let's step back for a minute so you can get the big picture and see where you are now. We started with acknowledging that today's workforce is incredibly diverse and that project managers must be sensitive to the cultural differences people bring to the team. Upon those two cornerstones we built a model for success. The model illustrates that daily interpersonal communication leads to stronger relationships. Those relationships cause feelings of trust, loyalty, commitment, and job satisfaction. These important emotions motivate people to work harder and be more productive, which ultimately leads to the project and sponsoring organization's success.

The most important implication of our Sequence for Success model is that project managers must facilitate open, honest, and frequent communication. "What?" you may ask. "If everyone's spending all their time talking, when are they going to get the job done?" While you may be tempted to tell team members to quiet down and get to work, discouraging them from interacting with you or with each other will backfire.

Companies that realize their workers are more productive if they have more social interaction are taking some simple steps to foster internal communication. Here are four examples. Bank of America observed that employees working in their call centers who had formed tight-knit communications groups were more productive and less likely to quit. To increase social communication, the bank introduced a shared 15-minute coffee break each day. Afterward, call-handling productivity increased more than 10 percent, and turnover declined nearly 70 percent.

In a second case, a pharmaceutical company replaced coffee makers used by a few marketing workers with a larger cafe area. The result? Increased sales and less turnover. A third example is a tech company. The workers who sat at larger tables in the cafeteria, thus communicating more, were found to be more productive than workers who sat at smaller tables.[14]

Adam Grant, an organizational psychologist, presents a fourth example company that facilitates communication in his book, *Give and Take: A Revolutionary Approach to Success*. Grant describes a large telecommunications firm in San Francisco. The professional engineers who worked at the firm were asked to rate themselves and each other on how much time they spent giving and receiving information from one another. The results reinforce the connection between communication and productivity. The engineers who gave the most help were the most productive and were held in the highest respect by their peers. By giving often, engineers built up more trust and attracted more cooperation from across their work groups, not just from the people they helped.[15]

In his book, Grant also tells how a former CEO at Deloitte improved his communication style. The executive, Jim Quigley, set a goal in meetings to talk no more than 20 percent of the time. "One of my objectives is listening. Many times you can have bigger impact if you know what to ask, rather than knowing what to say," Quigley explained. As he increased his questions, Quigley found himself gaining a deeper understanding of other people's needs.[16]

As you can see from these examples, simple steps such as arranging the work environment to facilitate communication and encouraging people to interact informally pays big dividends. Talking, listening, and asking questions are learning experiences. Enjoyable learning experiences. The more you learn about your team and the more they learn about each other, the easier it is for everyone to work together toward a common goal. That's the key to project management success.

> Talking, listening, and asking questions are learning experiences.

Summary

The basic premise of this chapter is carried throughout the book. Simply put, the premise is that communication is a key knowledge area for project managers from start to finish.

The *PMBOK® Guide* is identified as the primary resource for project managers. The organization of the Guide is explained, and the sections about the importance of communication in a project's life cycle are highlighted.

This chapter also introduces a conceptual model that is the framework for the book's premise—the Sequence for Success. Beginning with a description of the two cornerstones of diversity appreciation and cultural competence, the chapter shows that project communication should be frequent, open, and honest. Frequent, respectful interactions with team members and other stakeholders (level 2 of the model) will result in stronger work relationships (level 3). These relationships, in turn, will foster the key emotional conditions of trust, loyalty, commitment, and job satisfaction (level 4). People feeling these emotions are engaged in their work. They are motivated to work cooperatively, which leads to productivity and organizational success (level 5).

Questions

1. The *PMBOK® Guide—Sixth Edition* identifies ten key knowledge areas for project managers. List all ten and give an example of a process or activity the project manager must be able to perform, based on that knowledge area.

2. Explain how the *PMBOK® Guide—Sixth Edition* contributes to the effort to secure recognition for project management as a profession.

3. This chapter proposes that effective communication is critical at every phase of a project's life cycle. Select one phase—*initiating* or starting the project, *planning* or organizing and preparing, *executing* or carrying out the work, and *closing* or ending the project—and give an example of the communication behaviors that a project manager will engage in during that phase.

4. The Sequence for Success model has five levels, according to this chapter. Why do you think they appear in the sequence that they do? In other words, what is the rationale for this hierarchy?

CHAPTER 2

Communication Cornerstones

Chapter Objectives

The purpose of this chapter is to help project managers learn strategies and techniques for

- Communicating in agile and waterfall methods of project management
- Overcoming communication barriers
- Appreciating diversity
- Developing cultural competence

As explained in Chapter 1, communication is a key knowledge area for project managers. Chapter 2 begins by demonstrating the importance of communication in two typical methods of project management—agile and waterfall. In both methods, managers often face communication barriers. Overcoming these barriers is the focus of the second part of this chapter.

Next, the chapter lays two "cornerstones" or basic concepts that are the foundation on which the Sequence for Success model of project management, introduced in Chapter 1, is built. The first cornerstone is *diversity appreciation* (Figure 2.1). Given the increasing diversity of the workforce, it is crucial to recognize the competitive advantages that diversity offers. For our purposes, the term "diversity" encompasses differences in competencies, perspectives, and experience as well as in demographic characteristics such as gender, race, ethnicity, and age. The chapter also suggests several communication strategies that you, as a project manager, can adopt to capitalize on the advantages of workforce diversity.

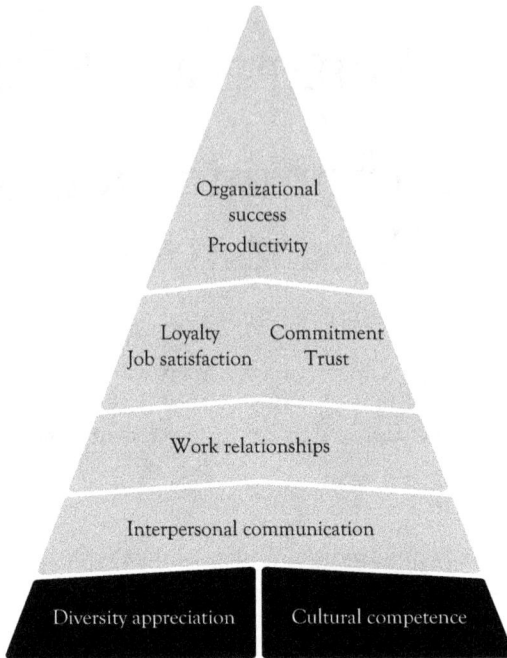

Figure 2.1 Cornerstones of the sequence for success

In the final section of this chapter the model's other cornerstone, *cultural competence,* is discussed (Figure 2.1). Diversity brings with it different cultural norms, leadership styles, and communication patterns, so you can see the critical link between cultural competence and your success as a project manager. If you know how to navigate among cultural differences, you will be equipped to develop positive relationships with your team, leading to productivity, profits, and organizational success.

Communicating in Agile and Waterfall Methods

Two basic approaches to project management have emerged in the recent literature—agile and waterfall. Both approaches are subsequently explained, in the context of a project's life cycle.

Project Life Cycles

In general, projects go through several stages as they progress from start to finish. These stages in the life cycle of a project are identified in the *Guide to the Project Management Body of Knowledge* as *initiating* or starting the project, *planning* or organizing and preparing, *executing* or carrying out the work, and *closing* or ending the project.[1]

One of the main differences among life cycles in projects pertains to how much uncertainty there is at the start of a project. If a project life cycle is predictable and plan-driven, the emphasis is on specifying requirements and details at the beginning of a project, then following the detailed plans. This style of management is often called *waterfall*. At the other extreme, if a project life cycle is unpredictable, the requirements emerge as the project progresses, and planning and executing are done iteratively. This style of management is often called *agile*.[2]

Project managers may choose to follow a *hybrid* management style, using waterfall style for the portions of the project that are predictable, easy to understand, and unlikely to change, then switching to the agile style for the portions of the project that are uncertain and/or likely to change considerably. Sometimes projects start out as waterfall but develop into agile as the level of complexity increases, unexpected events occur, and so on. Project managers need to be flexible enough to be able to "shift gears" as appropriate. Each project management method is described in more detail next, and the importance of good communication in each method is identified.

Stages in a Project's Life Cycle:

1. Initiating
2. Planning
3. Executing
4. Closing

Waterfall Project Management

If you are managing a project that you are comfortable with and that has a high level of predictability to it, then the traditional or "waterfall" management style is appropriate. That is, the project begins with a clear goal and a detailed plan. As you and your team follow the plan and move through the stages of the project's life cycle, you experience a low level of uncertainty. You are confident that a successful outcome will result from following the prescribed steps in the process.

Here is an example of a project for which waterfall management may be most appropriate. You are the president of the Booster Club for your child's high school marching band. The project is a fundraiser, the proceeds of which will go toward new band uniforms. As a seasoned veteran of fundraising projects, you are confident about the steps that will be necessary, as well as their sequence. All the other band parents (stakeholders) know and respect your expertise. The band director and the school principal (project sponsors) have pledged their support. Everyone is grateful to you for taking the lead on this project. The parents are eager to pitch in and help raise money for the much-needed uniforms, and their children have volunteered too. They are likely to follow your directives, meet deadlines, and accomplish their tasks.

Consistent, clear, open communication is key at every stage of the project, so formal channels are established to expedite information flow. Formal channels are also thought of as official media. The channels are both *oral*, such as meetings and teleconferences with the other parents and the sponsors, and *written*, such as progress reports, posters, e-mails, a webpage for the fundraiser on the school's website, and flowcharts. As the Booster Club president, you are comfortable with a directive approach throughout the stages of the fundraiser's life cycle—you update the sponsors at each stage, you delegate work to the parents according to their strengths and talents, you check that deadlines are met, you broadcast news of the fundraiser throughout the school and community, and you ensure that all the communication channels stay open. Your waterfall management method is likely to result in the project's success.

Agile Project Management

Agile means "the ability to move quickly and easily." The aim of agility is adaptivity, the responsive capacity to adapt to new requirements: to be ready for anything. Although all projects begin with a plan and a goal, some projects have a high degree of uncertainty throughout their life cycles, which requires that the team move in unexpected directions at each stage. Detailed plans emerge as the project progresses, one bit at a time.

According to Mike Hoogveld, author of *Agile Management*, agility is based on eight key principles:

1. ***Creating value***—The highest priority is value for both internal and external customers through rapid and continuous delivery of new or renewed products and services.
2. ***Understanding the customer***—In order to create value for the target group, it is necessary to understand their requirements, needs, and behaviors.
3. ***Alignment***—Creating value for the customer requires that the customer is given a central position in the close collaboration of a team of stakeholders from all relevant departments.
4. ***Empowerment***—The team should get all the support and autonomy it needs, removing any external obstacles and giving it the full trust and mandate to do the job independently.

Principles of Agile Management:

1. Creating value
2. Understanding the customer
3. Alignment
4. Empowerment
5. Synchronous and visual communication
6. Learning by experimenting
7. Speed and flexibility
8. Accountability

---

5. ***Synchronous and visual communication***—The most efficient and effective way to share information with or within the team is via synchronous communication, preferably face-to-face.
6. ***Learning by experimenting***—The most important measure of progress is learning via a structured cycle, and this requires accurate measurement. Experimentation and failure form an important part of learning.

7. *Speed and flexibility*—Change should be considered as a source of opportunity, because the ability to respond quickly to changes is a source of competitive advantage.

8. *Accountability*—The team should be accountable. After each iteration, the team honestly evaluates all its actions and results, adjusting its plans and activities accordingly.[3]

Reading through these eight principles, you can see that good communication is as crucial for agile management as it is for the waterfall management method. One major distinction, however, is that the agile approach calls for less direction from the manager. In particular, the fourth principle, empowerment, requires that the manager step back and simply provide daily opportunities for the team to interact informally, brainstorm solutions, and identify processes on their own. Agile management requires trust, of course. Chapter 4 presents strategies for developing trust within the team as well as between the project manager and the team, thereby ensuring project success.

Here is an example of a project for which agile management may be most appropriate. You are a member of your child's elementary school Parents and Teachers Organization (PTO). At the most recent meeting a parent suggested that an after school program would help working parents who can't be home when the school bus drops off their children in the afternoon. There is enough agreement among the other parents attending the meeting that a committee is formed to look into establishing an after school program. You are elected to be the committee chair, or project leader.

You want to use agile management as the project team (called the PTO After School Program Committee) pursues their charge. You launch by making sure that the project's goal has been clarified and an overall plan has been agreed on. Then you step back, allowing the others to organize and perform activities as they see fit, make decisions, solve problems, and move through the life cycle stages without strong direction from you. Instead, you focus on facilitating, encouraging, providing resources, and above all, keeping the communication flowing. Figure 2.2 illustrates the communication activities that are emphasized in agile management.

Figure 2.2 Communication goals in agile project management

As you review Figure 2.2 you will notice that *informal* communication has been added to the various channels for *formal* communication that the waterfall method calls for. As we have seen, waterfall management methods rely mostly on formal, highly structured communication channels. These channels, such as written reports and e-mail, are archivable and searchable. Because the messages conveyed on these channels are permanent, they provide stability to the project.

By contrast, agile management methods rely more on informal, loosely structured communications. Agile project managers often find that motivating, managing conflicts and interpersonal issues, building cohesiveness, creating synergy and similar responsibilities are best accomplished when communicating one-to-one in informal conversations with stakeholders—Hoogveld's fifth principle. The American business magnate, T. Boone Pickens, agrees. He famously said, "Keep things informal. Talking is the natural way to do business....Talk generates ideas. Great things come from luncheon meetings which consist of a sandwich, a cup of soup, and a good idea or two."

Talking is the natural way to do business....Talk generates ideas.

Overcoming Communication Barriers

Whether a project manager decides to apply waterfall, agile, or hybrid methods, communication is crucial for success. A range of oral and written, formal and informal, communication channels must be established and maintained throughout the project's life cycle. In doing so, managers often face communication barriers. Overcoming these barriers is the focus of the following part of this chapter.

Barriers to Cultural Competence

The biggest roadblock to communication competence is our own cultural values. From an early age we are taught that our views of the world are correct, and everyone who sees things differently is wrong. This bias against difference is natural and normal, not pathological, and mostly subconscious. But every day our biases determine what we see and how we judge those around us. We have biases about almost every dimension of human identity.

> Bias is a normal psychological reaction to difference.

The Halo Effect. Bias is a barrier because it distorts people's perceptions, so we tend to see and hear only what we want to see and hear. The most prevalent source of bias is the halo effect, which managers fall prey to when they allow the evaluation of one characteristic to be influenced by another characteristic or by a general impression. One aspect of the project or workplace may affect the manager's impression of the project team members in other areas. For instance, if a team member is habitually prompt, the project manager could let this characteristic influence her impression of the team member's other, unrelated abilities such as technical competency.

The Recency Effect. Another source of bias is the recency effect. This occurs when the latest information disproportionately affects all the earlier information. For example, if a team member unexpectedly begins struggling with a new task, the project manager might begin to doubt the quality of her work on previously assigned tasks.

Sources of Bias:

- Halo effect
- Recency effect
- Opinion leaders
- Preconceived attitudes
- Trigger words
- Perceived similarities

Opinion Leaders. A third source of bias is the opinions of respected others. Project managers frequently are influenced by stakeholders' and sponsors' opinions. For instance, if a project manager is told, "You'll get nothing but trouble from Patrick, but you'll find Semkins easy to work with," and then Patrick complains to the manager about a missing piece of data, the manager might label Patrick a whiner who compares unfavorably with Semkins, who "never complains." Smart managers wait to form their own impressions of team members.

Preconceived Attitudes. Managers' personal biases may have a drastic effect on the outcome of an interaction. Managers who are unaware of personal bias may become selective in what they pay attention to. They may deal only with preconceived notions and even debate with others on points of disagreement. For example, a manager who believes that young adults are generally unreliable may disregard any information indicating that a particular young team member *is* reliable.

Trigger Words. Emotional words or phrases can also trigger bias. Such phrases as "typical humorless accountant," "it really isn't my job," "that'll never work," or "all engineers think alike" can lead to emotional responses. The danger in such phrases is that they cause a listener to attend (or not to attend) to different parts of a message.

Perceived Similarities. We are attracted to and tend to like people who are similar to us, not different from us. The perceived similarities may or may not be real. When people think they're similar, they expect to have positive future interactions. Therefore, the discovery of similarities and differences is crucial in developing work relationships. Here's an example:

You are interviewing candidates for your project team. When a candidate walks in and greets you, you immediately notice her gender, race, dress, appearance, speech patterns, handshake, even body size. And you immediately form judgments based on those outward factors. If you perceive those factors to be similar to yours, you probably form a positive impression of the candidate. On the other hand, if you perceive those factors to be different from yours, you probably form a negative impression. As the interview goes along and you gain more information about her background, experiences, and skills, you probably will pay most attention to the information that confirms your first impressions and disregard the information that conflicts with them. That normal mental process can lead to bias and discrimination. It can also lead to costly staffing decisions.

Overcoming the Barriers to Cultural Competence

How can you avoid scenarios like the one shown earlier? Research has found that people who try hard can control their bias. Howard Ross, the founder of Cook Ross, an international diversity consulting company and author of *Everyday Bias* and *Reinventing Diversity*, suggests four strategies for developing cultural competence:

1. ***Recognize and accept that you have biases.*** Bias is a normal psychological phenomenon. Rather than feel guilty about your biases, take responsibility for them. Once you accept them, you can begin to limit their impact.
2. ***Practice "constructive uncertainty."*** Slow down decision making, especially when it affects other people.
3. ***Try to interact regularly with and learn about people you feel biased against.*** Exposing yourself to positive role models will reduce the risk of discrimination.
4. ***Look at how you make decisions.*** Consider the impact of environmental factors, time of day, and your physical and emotional state in order to identify barriers to perception.[4]

Strategies for Developing Cultural Competence:

1. Recognize and accept that you have biases.
2. Practice constructive uncertainty.
3. Learn about people you feel biased against.
4. Look at how you make decisions.

Let's apply Ross's four strategies to the team interview scenario described earlier. If your first impression of the candidate is negative because you perceived her outward characteristics (age, appearance, race, gender, voice, handshake) to be different from yours, what should you do? First, recognize your bias and the possibility of premature judgment. Next, deliberately decide that you won't jump to conclusions. Ask questions and listen closely to her responses. Try to penetrate well below the surface so you can exchange information more accurately. Bring in another interviewer whose opinions you respect and then compare impressions afterward.

While it's true that similarities make it easy to build relationships at work, different traits and outlooks will give your team balance, opportunities for growth, and possibilities for learning new ways of thinking. In the words of Pat Wadors, Head of Human Resources at LinkedIn, "When we listen and celebrate what is both common and different, we become a wiser, more inclusive, and better organization." Becoming aware of your mental processes will help you to become culturally competent so you can make better decisions, whether it's about selecting members for your project team or anything else.

"When we…celebrate what is both common and different, we become a wiser, more inclusive, and better organization."

Communicating Across Cultures

Today's project managers will often find themselves working with culturally diverse teams, which makes it imperative that they develop competence in communicating across cultures. Managers can develop cultural sensitivity without actually living or working in other cultures. After all, managing diversity successfully brings high value to all contemporary organizations, not just multinational organizations. Despite the fact that diverse workforces are the norm, a 2013 Towers Watson Global Workforce Study shows that only about half of managers are viewed as effective at bridging differences among their teams.[5]

Managers who try to treat all employees fairly and respectfully may encounter common pitfalls. In an attempt to communicate interculturally, they may try ignoring differences. Or they may decide that cultural sensitivity requires treating each person differently. Thus, at one extreme, a manager may take the *universalist* approach by treating all employees the same. At the other extreme, a manager may take the *particularist* approach, adjusting the treatment according to the worker's culture. However, Michael Morris, a business professor at Columbia University, says that both approaches can have a negative effect on employees' perception of justice. "If justice issues are not well-managed in a diverse workplace, detrimental consequences ranging from poor morale and turnover to intergroup rivalry and balkanization may result."[6]

Morris offers 10 ways managers can overcome cultural differences when communicating:

1. Rely on multiethnic strategies, not just on good intentions.
2. Provide all team members with constructive feedback so they learn and grow.
3. Work to ensure that all team members have access to opportunities.
4. Work to ensure that all team members perceive that they are treated fairly.
5. Provide cultural competence training.
6. Monitor cultural boundaries to avoid engendering intergroup competition.
7. Manage misunderstandings by making team members aware that cultural differences may be the root cause of clashes rather than personality differences.
8. Be sensitive to obstacles facing members of certain cultural groups.

9. Call on those with cultural expertise if you recognize a problem brewing within the team.
10. Include all team members in diversity discussions.

Let's apply some of Morris's strategies to a common situation involving culturally diverse teams—the value of certain rewards and benefits to different age groups. There are distinct differences between generations of workers regarding what they find rewarding. Older workers are more likely to believe that money is the primary motivator for workplace behavior. However, in a recent survey of over one thousand small business owners, Bank of America found that among younger workers quality of life is as important, if not more important, than money. More than 80 percent of the survey's participants said they offer benefits including flexible hours, training and professional development, and the chance to work at a location they choose.[7]

> "People seem to generally value time and flexibility over prestige or money."
> —Jens Jakob Andersen, CEO, RunRepeat.com

A culturally sensitive project manager who applies Morris's strategies does not assume that all team members will find the same reward equally valuable, and therefore discusses options with each member to determine what they prefer regarding time, flexibility, and monetary benefits.

In summary, cultural competence has taken on great significance, both in recruitment and retention of multicultural workers. Managing diversity is every manager's challenge. Project managers help develop a welcoming culture that values individuals regardless of culture, intellect, talents, gender, or age. Strong communication skills help managers connect with others in a deep and direct way to develop relationships that bridge differences.

Appreciating Diversity

If you're at work right now, take a look at the people on your team. There's Ben, who's still a PC person, despite your repeated attempts to show him the superiority of a Mac. There's Isabelle, who irritates you because she's so closed-minded and stubborn about politics. Over there is Joey, who refuses to agree that *Star Wars* is the all-time greatest blockbuster movie series.

You probably don't have a whole lot in common with any of the people you work with. The workplace is a loose affiliation of people with widely different religions, political preferences, worldviews, backgrounds, and interests. Maybe you've formed a little tribe of likeminded people with whom you can relax over lunch and discuss Sunday's game. If so, you probably think that work would be lots easier if only these people were on your team instead of the others.

This section of Chapter 2 proposes that workplace pluralism is not only a fact of life, it's a competitive advantage. As the Sequence for Success model shows, diversity appreciation is a cornerstone for project success (Figure 2.1). Further, this section presents strategies that you, as a project manager, can adopt to capitalize on the advantages and minimize the disadvantages of workforce diversity. The trick is not to work *against* your team members' differences, but to work *with* them for project success. Finally, this section suggests ways you can improve your communication competence when interacting with two particularly tricky populations on the job: age-diverse and gender-diverse workers.

Benefits of Workplace Diversity

If you're a tough, skeptical manager in this values-obsessed age, you've probably asked yourself, "Why should I do anything special to 'embrace diversity'?" There are some good answers to your question. Of the important reasons that managers should leverage diversity, two are undeniable—diversity fosters innovative solutions and improves performance.

Benefits of Diversity:

- Innovative solutions
- Superior performance

More Innovative Solutions. Francis Bacon, a 15th century philosopher and father of the scientific method, said, "Those who will not apply new remedies must expect new evils, for time is the greatest innovator." Teams working in the global economy must rely on diverse thinkers who can create innovative solutions to new problems. Diversity is a competitive advantage because different people approach similar problems in different ways. Thus, diverse teams make better decisions.

Morgan Stanley is an example of a company that fosters diversity in its workforce because they recognize that diverse workgroups are better at creative problem solving. Jeff Brodsky, Chief Human Resources officer, said, "We believe a diverse workforce brings innovative thinking and enables us to serve our clients in a way that delivers the best financial solutions."[8]

Superior Performance. A second benefit of project team diversity is improved performance. Government agencies came to that realization early. One example of a federal government agency that fosters diversity to enhance performance effectiveness is the National Aeronautics and Space Administration (NASA). The team that developed Rover, the device that crawled around the surface of Mars as part of the Mars Pathfinder Mission in 2000, exhibited true diversity. The 20-person team included three women, one African American male, and an East Indian male, according to Donna Shirley, Head of the Mars Pathfinder Mission. Speaking at an Innovative Thinking Conference in Scottsdale, Arizona, Shirley described the team as being diverse on other dimensions as well, including thinking style, experience, creativity, and personality. She pointed out that the diversity of talents enabled the Pathfinder project to fulfill its mission with a budget of $264 million, "roughly the budget for the film, 'Waterworld.' And it got better reviews."

> Diversity is good for the bottom line.

Multinational corporations agree with nonprofits and governmental agencies that diversity is linked to performance. What began for many companies as an effort to meet governmental and legal requirements has evolved into a strategic priority for success. Businesses with a committed, long-term, systematic, and strategic approach to diversity consistently show better performance.[9] As Sundar Pichai, CEO of Google, points out, "A diverse mix of voices leads to better discussions, decisions, and outcomes for everyone."

Ford Motor Company is an example of a corporation that has created metrics to prove the impact of diversity initiatives on the company's overall business strategy. At Ford, for instance, employee resource groups (ERGs) demonstrate their value to the bottom line by tracking the number of vehicles members sell through the company's Friends and Neighbors vehicle discount plan. Michele Jayne, Personnel Research Manager for Ford, said, "Achieving a diverse workforce and effectively managing this workforce can yield huge benefits."[10]

Simply put, diversity is good for the bottom line.

Strategies for Welcoming and Supporting Diversity

Project managers can take concrete actions to foster diversity appreciation. Here are three strategies for welcoming diversity to your project teams.

Ways to Support Diversity:

- Recruit diverse employees
- Establish employee support groups
- Establish mentorship programs

Recruit Diverse Employees. Massachusetts Mutual Life Insurance Company and Morgan Stanley are companies that strive to reach out to community partners and to recruit and retain workforces that incorporate a range of cultures, backgrounds, experiences, and perspectives. Both businesses actively recruit talent from historically underrepresented backgrounds and communities. Recruiters search for potential employees as early as high school. They partner with prestigious universities, campus diversity groups, and other organizations committed to diversity, such as the National Association of Black Accountants.

Establish Employee Support Groups. Prudential is a company that creates and supports employee networks whose charge is to promote social activities and professional development. Among the groups is "VetNet," for active members of the military, veterans, and veterans' partners. Another is the "Employee Association of Gay Men, Lesbians, Bisexuals, Transgenders, and Allies (EAGLES)," a group that helped conduct research on the financial and legal concerns of same-sex couples and LGBTQ parents.

Establish Mentorship Programs. As support groups for employees of similar backgrounds, MassMutual's ERGs provide mentoring. Syvaria Echevarria values her Latina ERG. "I never thought I'd be in the position I am today because there weren't people around me when I was growing up who worked in a professional setting that I could look to share experiences," she says.

"Morgan Stanley is very much an apprenticeship culture," says Jeff Brodsky, Chief HR officer. Among their mentoring programs is "Return to Work," a 12-week paid internship, pairing participants with senior-level leaders based on their skills, experiences, and interests.

Comprehensive apprenticeships are available that include skills development, stretch assignments, mentoring and coaching for women and minorities.

Communicating with Diverse Workers

Once you've recognized that workplace diversity contributes important advantages to an organization and you've identified ways that you can welcome and support a pluralistic team environment, you may be wondering how all of this affects your daily communication patterns. After all, the purpose of this book is to help you improve your project communication skills.

Age Diversity. Americans are living longer, and the average employee is getting older. For the first time ever, four generations are working together. These groups include the shrinking sector of Silents who are in their 70s but still working, the large post-World War II Boomer generation, Gen-Xers born in the late '60s to about 1980, and Millennials born after 1980. Every generation is different, and generation gaps are natural.

If you are a Gen Xer or a Millennial, you may well find yourself managing a team of people old enough to be your parents or even your grandparents. How awkward is that?

Boomers aren't yet ready to step aside, and they expect their younger managers and team mates to respect them for their age and experience. If you manage a team of older employees, here are some communication tips:

- Get at the roots of the problem rather than working from assumptions
- Be specific about inappropriate behaviors; don't generalize or stereotype
- Allow the team members to vent and express themselves
- Demonstrate empathy

Think of ways to capitalize on their life experience by offering mentoring opportunities and special assignments. To help keep their skills up to date, provide more job sharing, job rotation, and training. Working in teams with varied ages allows everyone to develop respect for other's strengths and worldviews.

Strategies for Managing Older Workers:

- Mentoring opportunities
- Special assignments
- Job sharing
- Short-term projects
- Job rotation
- Training

Now let's briefly look at the reverse situation—managers in charge of a team from a younger generation. According to Harvard Business School researchers, Unlike Boomers, Gen Xersoften expect to be evaluated for productivity, not hours at their desk, especially when tech tools make their geographic location irrelevant. Their loyalties lie with their social network rather than their job, and they do not fear change.

Strategies for Managing Younger Workers:

- Flextime
- Focus on goals, not methods
- Technology tools
- Variety
- Long-term projects

By 2020, fully half of the U.S. workforce will consist of Millennials. Their values and attitudes are already manifesting in interesting workplace changes. For instance, new corporate office buildings are designed for maximum natural light, with high ceilings, outdoor areas, and common spaces rather than small offices and cubicles. The emphasis is on "we" space rather than "me" space.[11] Companies such as ExxonMobil and Anadarko currently provide amenities such as fitness centers, jogging trails, bicycle racks, and wellness centers to attract and keep younger employees.

Clearly, when values clash between managers and project teams, effective communication across the generational divide becomes even more important. Project managers must be sensitive to age diversity because of its implications for employee retention, harmony, and team efficiency.

Gender Diversity. Over the past 30 years, researchers have closely examined how men and women communicate differently at work, but results have been inconsistent because of the complexity of contributing factors. Social scientist Deborah Tannen not only found strong evidence for gender differences but made a case for supporting the differences in communication styles of men and women.[12] Some of the gender differences in workplace conversations that Tannen identified are shown in Table 2.1.

Table 2.1 illustrates that differences often exist between men and women as to how they handle various communication situations. In addition to these differences in speaking styles, researchers also have identified

Table 2.1 Men and women in conversation

Men	Example	Women	Example
Asks for information	Who's the expert on this software?	Asks for help	I need help learning this software.
Uses report-talk	These are the facts.	Uses rapport-talk	Most of us are happy with this solution.
Uses powerful language	That won't work.	Uses powerless language	I may be wrong, and stop me if you disagree, but I think there may be roadblocks.
Complains	Because you missed a deadline the project's schedule is wrecked.	Apologizes	I'm sorry to hear that you can't meet the deadline.

differences in listening styles. Women are more likely to listen to affirm both the relationship and the person who is speaking, zooming in on an emotional level and being empathic. In contrast, men tend to listen for the facts and information in a message and are less comfortable handling its emotional content. They are more likely to listen for solutions and are more willing to give advice than empathy.[13]

Such differences in communication style between genders don't appear to be diminishing, and they are important because of the increasing gender diversity of the workforce. According to Sheryl Sandberg, COO of Facebook and author of the bestseller, *Lean In*, companies with more gender diversity have more revenue, customers, market share, and profits.[14] Both men and women will experience more professional success if they apply the communication strategies presented here.

Developing Cultural Competence

Corporate response to the increasing diversity of the workforce varies widely, but cultural competence is generally valued. Indeed, today's organizations consider intercultural skills as a top consideration when hiring. In a recent survey of 318 executives from both private sector and non-profit organizations, 96 percent agreed that it's mandatory for their new hires to be "comfortable working with colleagues and customers from diverse cultural backgrounds."[15]

Reactions to Diversity in Business:

1. Affirmative action
2. Inclusion
3. Cultural competence

Briefly, a culturally competent manager understands that culture profoundly affects workplace behavior and attitudes. Look again at the Sequence for Success model to see that cultural competence is one of the cornerstones for project success (Figure 2.1). Furthermore, a culturally competent manager knows how to navigate relevant cultural differences in order to maximize workers' loyalty, satisfaction, productivity, and ultimately the bottom line. *The Economist* Intelligence Unit recently surveyed 572 executives in multinational organizations around the globe. The business leaders overwhelmingly agreed that cultural competence improves revenues (89 percent), profits (89 percent), and market share (85 percent). The executives widely agreed that managerial communication skills are essential for workforce productivity.[16]

Why Culture Matters

Let's take a closer look at the notion of culture so we can see why it's such an important factor in managerial success. Culture is what we grow up in. Beginning in childhood, we learn acceptable behaviors, customs, and habits. We also adopt the beliefs, values, and moral attitudes of the society in which we mature. A body of common understanding develops.

Culture is what we grow up in.

Malcolm Gladwell explored the importance of culture in his bestseller, *Outliers: The Story of Success*. He concluded that "cultural legacies are powerful forces. They have deep roots and long lives. They persist, generation after generation, virtually intact …and we cannot make sense of our world without them."[17]

A Closer Look at Cultural Differences

What are the "deep roots" of cultural differences that Gladwell was refer-
ring to? One of the most extensive studies of cultural differences was
conducted at IBM Corporation by a Dutch management thinker, Geert
Hofstede. He surveyed more than 116,000 IBM employees in 40 countries. A massive statistical analysis of his findings revealed six dimensions
of national culture as shown in Table 2.2: power distance, uncertainty
avoidance, individualism/collectivism, masculinity/femininity, high and
low context, and monochronic/polychronic time.[18] Examining Hofstede's
framework can help you anticipate and then solve possible problems
caused by misunderstandings between team members from different
cultures.

Table 2.2 Hofstede's dimensions of cultural differences

High power distance	←——————→	Low power distance
High uncertainty avoidance	←——————→	Low uncertainty avoidance
Collectivism	←——————→	Individualism
Masculinity	←——————→	Femininity
High context	←——————→	Low context
Polychronic time	←——————→	Monochronic time

Power distance indicates the extent to which a society accepts the fact
that power is distributed unequally. It is reflected in the values of both
the more powerful and less powerful members of the society. According
to Hofstede's research, the Philippines, Venezuela, and Mexico are countries with high power distance; and Denmark, New Zealand, the United
States, and Israel are a few of the countries with low power distance.

High/Low Power Distance: the extent to which society accepts the
unequal distribution of power.

If you are managing team members from a culture with high power
distance they might address you respectfully by title and surname and
expect a controlling strategy from you. On the other hand, if you are from
a culture with a lower power distance, you may think of yourself as having

little more power than the team members, expecting them to behave pro-actively and to communicate in more equalitarian style.

Uncertainty avoidance relates to the degree to which a society feels threatened by uncertainty and by ambiguous situations. People within such a society try to avoid these uncertainties and ambiguous situations by providing greater career stability, establishing and following formal rules, discouraging odd ideas and behaviors, and believing in absolute truths and the attainment of expertise. Greece, Germany, England, and Japan are said to have strong uncertainty avoidance, while Hong Kong, Denmark, the United States, and Sweden are said to have weak uncertainty avoidance.

> High/Low Uncertainty Avoidance: the extent to which society feels threatened by ambiguity.

If you are managing team members whose culture values uncertainty avoidance, you may have difficulty getting them to embrace change. Typically, they will prefer the status quo. To reduce resistance, try to get your people involved in the new strategy and highlight the benefits of change.

On the *individualism/collectivism* dimension, *individualism* suggests a loosely knit social framework in which people are expected to take care of themselves and their immediate families only. *Collectivism,* on the other hand, is a tight social framework in which people distinguish between in-groups and out-groups. They expect their in-group (relatives, clan, organization) to take care of them; and because of that, they believe they owe absolute loyalty to their in-group. The United States, Australia, and Great Britain are the most highly individualistic countries on Hofstede's scale, while Pakistan, Colombia, Nigeria, and Venezuela are more collectivist countries.

> Individualism/Collectivism: the extent to which society prefers loyalty to the group over loyalty to the individual.

If you are a manager from an individualistic culture with a team from a collectivist culture, you may become frustrated when they resist making decisions. They must first collaborate to reach consensus. Try to be patient while the members spend what you consider excessive time in conference.

Masculinity/femininity is the fourth Hofstede dimension. Masculinity includes assertiveness, the acquisition of money and things, and not caring about the quality of life. These values are labeled masculine because, within nearly all societies studied by Hofstede's researchers, men scored higher in these values than women. Japan, Austria, and Mexico were among the most masculine societies. Feminine cultures, by contrast, value family, children, and quality of life. Denmark, Sweden, and Norway are considered feminine cultures.

Masculinity/Femininity: the extent to which society values quality of life.

If you are a project manager who identifies with Hofstede's masculine values and whose team includes people who embrace Hofstede's feminine values, they will appreciate your engaging in conversations about personal aspects of their lives and participating in non-work-related celebrations such as birthdays.

Context is the fifth cultural difference in Hofstede's model. In a *high-context* culture, much information is gathered from the physical context or environment or the person's behavior. People look for meaning in what is not said—in the nonverbal communication or body language; in the silences, the facial expressions, and the gestures. Japan and Saudi Arabia are high-context countries according to Hofstede's model, as are Chinese-and Spanish-speaking countries.

High/Low Context: the extent to which society gathers information from the environment.

In a *low-context* culture, the most information comes from the language. In such a culture, communicators emphasize sending and receiving accurate messages directly, usually by being highly articulate. Canada and the United States are low-context cultures as defined by Hofstede's model.

If you are managing a high-context team, pay careful attention to your nonverbal behaviors, as the team members are likely to read more into these behaviors than into your words.

Monochronic v. polychronic time is the sixth dimension of cultural differences, according to Hofstede. In a monochronic culture, such as Germany, the United States, and most westernized nations, we talk about saving time, wasting time, making time, and spending time. We measure time by the clock, often in nanoseconds. In hyper-punctual countries like Japan, pedestrians walk fast and bank clocks are accurate. In Western businesses we read quarterly returns and define "long-term" projections as those going out three to five years into the future.

Monochronic/Polychronic: the way a society perceives time.

In polychronic cultures, such as Spain, Latin America, and most Asian countries, time is not linear. Time is measured by events, not the clock. Thus, promptness diminishes in value, and being "late" is a sign of status. People in polychronic cultures are more patient, less interested in time management or measurement, and more willing to wait for their rewards than those in monochronic cultures.

If your project team embraces monochronic values, they will expect you to begin and end meetings on time, provide resources when promised, and enforce deadlines throughout the project's life cycle.

Developing Cultural Competence

Now that we have used Hofstede's model to explore the deep roots of some cultural differences, you can see that culture has a profound effect on each of us. As a culturally competent project manager, you will recognize that culture determines why your team members may

- prefer authoritarian or democratic leadership
- need more or less personal space and privacy
- perceive punctuality as important or not
- are future-oriented or look to the past
- are factual or intuitive in decision making

- value individual achievement or loyalty to the group
- focus only on the words or on everything except the words

Once you recognize how pervasive a person's culture is and how different it may be from yours, you can then begin to appreciate the complexity of good management. You will see and accept things as others see and accept them because you want your culturally diverse team to succeed.

Culture and Communication Style

At this point you may be thinking, "The concept of cultural competence is pretty abstract. What are some concrete actions I can take to enhance my cultural competence and help the project team to succeed?"

The answer is that cultural competence is reflected in your communication style. Every day, when you interact with coworkers, subordinates, customers, suppliers, and other stakeholders, everyone's culture acts as a lens through which your messages are filtered. Similarly, their messages to you are filtered through your own cultural lens. Being sensitive to unintended distortions of the messages' meanings equals cultural competence.

Cultural competence is reflected in communication style.

Cultural Sources of Communication Breakdown. Various cultures view feedback differently. For example, managers in the United States and Europe typically prefer direct communication; they deliver feedback that is explicit, honest, and authentic. In Asian cultures, communication is expected to be more vague and indirect, and managerial feedback is more likely to be nuanced because bluntness might injure the employees' self-esteem. Furthermore, Asian cultures value silence. Silence, like talk, communicates.[19]

Cultural Sources of Misunderstanding in Conversations:

- Degree of directness
- Silence

- Loudness and pitch
- Appropriate topics
- Touch
- Eye contact

Here is an example of communication style differences that are culturally-based. A Chinese team member is speaking to the English project manager:

Chinese team member: My mother is not well, ma'am.
English project manager: So?
Chinese team member: She has to go into the hospital.
English project manager: That's too bad.
Chinese team member: On Thursday, ma'am.

The meaning of this exchange is clouded by cultural differences in communication style. The Chinese team member is hoping that her manager will realize what she wants and offer this before she has to ask for it. In British English, however, it is more typical to start with the request and then give reasons if required. So, the English version of this conversation would be something like this:

Chinese team member: Could I take a day off please?
English project manager: Why?
Chinese team member: My mother is not well and must go to the hospital on Thursday.

Typical British English speech patterns are similar to U.S. patterns in their degree of directness. When people from Asian cultures are more indirect, Westerners may view them as evasive. A Westerner lacking cultural competence might impatiently prod the speaker to "get to the point." On the other hand, a culturally competent Westerner would understand that the Asian roundabout pattern is used to avoid the risk of hurt feelings and is therefore often a more relationship-sensitive communication style.

Naoki Kameda, a prominent Japanese business communication researcher, explains that the indirect communication style represents important values, based on the "3Hs":

- Humanity—warm consideration for others
- Harmony—efforts not to hurt the feelings of others
- Humility—modesty[20]

By comparison, a direct style seems pretty self-centered, doesn't it?

Communication Style and Empathy. It's easier to communicate with others when you understand and agree with the cultural values behind their communication style preferences. Furthermore, if you can empathize with the other person, share their feelings and relate to their intentions, then you might even adopt their communication style during the interaction. All you have to do is ask yourself, "If I were on the receiving end, how would I react to this message?" Then adjust your communication style so the receiver's understanding is closer to what you intended. As you will read in Chapter 4, effective project communication leads to stronger relationships and feelings of empathy and trust. These emotional conditions, in turn, lead to improved performance, productivity, and organizational success.

Summary

The first cornerstone of communication competence in today's diverse workplace is recognition of its benefits. Major benefits of a diverse project team include stronger stakeholder connections, more innovative solutions, superior performance, and values-driven policies.

Along with diversity appreciation, cultural competence is a cornerstone for project success. Culturally competent managers understand that culture profoundly affects team behaviors and attitudes, and they know how to navigate relevant cultural differences in order to maximize team members' loyalty, satisfaction, productivity, and the bottom line.

While bias against differences is natural and normal, it can restrict thinking and prevent the development of workplace relationships, empathy, and trust. Culturally competent managers recognize that culture is a lens that filters messages. They develop flexible communication styles to overcome barriers and increase shared meaning.

Questions

1. Think of a project you managed or intend to manage. Which management method, agile or waterfall, seems the most appropriate? How could you apply it at each stage of the project's life cycle?

2. Select one of the six sources of bias presented in this chapter that has particular relevance to your project management experience. Analyze how bias was a communication barrier and identify a communication strategy that would have overcome it.

3. Which of the strategies for welcoming and supporting diversity that are described in this chapter seems to have the most benefit to your project team? What specific steps could you take to foster diversity appreciation in your team?

4. Hofstede identified six dimensions of cultural difference. Map one or two of them against your team's communication preferences. For instance, do you think that high power distance cultures prefer oral or written communication channels? What about high context cultures?

CHAPTER 3

Formal Interpersonal Communication

Chapter Objectives

The purpose of this chapter is to help project managers learn strategies and techniques for the following formal interpersonal communication situations:

- Receiving formal communications—listening, responding, and asking questions
- Communicating performance expectations—the Tell-Show-Do method, and designing formal training programs
- Delivering negative information and corrective feedback
- Giving positive performance feedback
- Conducting formal performance reviews
- Managing conflict

Receiving Formal Communications

When you're on the receiving end of a communication between you and a team member, an inappropriate reaction may end the interaction prematurely. This section presents three strategies for keeping the communication channels open, so you can stay informed. The strategies are listening, responding, and asking questions. These strategies are especially critical when the information coming your way is negative. Applying the strategies also will strengthen your rapport with the speaker.

Listening

As a project manager, you probably spend half to two-thirds of your time listening, yet 75 to 90 percent of what you hear is probably ignored, misunderstood, or forgotten.[1] That's because listening is hard work. It's not a passive experience. Your brain is not a sponge that absorbs whatever comes along. Listening is also difficult when you're busy and distracted with work. Your brain can think at least four times faster than anyone can talk, so while you're waiting for someone to get to the point, you've mentally moved on.

Listening requires active participation in the conversation. To create a healthy work atmosphere you have to keep the communication channels open. Begin by preparing yourself—both physically and psychologically—to listen.

Preparation Steps for Listening:

1. Pick the best place
2. Pick the best time
3. Think about personal biases
4. Consider listening styles
5. Establish a range of channels

---

1. *Pick the best possible place.* While it is not always possible to change the interaction's location, don't overlook better facilities when available. Selecting the best place helps reduce internal and external noise. Characteristics of a locale that maximizes listening include safety, security, privacy, and neutrality.

2. *Pick the best possible time.* As with place, it is not always possible to change the time. However, because time influences the psychological barriers of motivation, emotion, and willingness, deciding when to meet may significantly alter the conversation's outcome. When listening to virtual team members, be mindful of time zone differences, too.

3. *Think about personal biases* that may be present. If you are unaware of personal bias, you may become selective and hear only what you want to hear. Emotional words can also trigger listener bias. Such comments as "we tried that before, and it didn't work," or "all IT people think alike" can lead to emotional responses. The danger in

such comments is that they cause a listener to pay attention only to certain parts of a message. Don't let bias distract you from understanding the message.

4. ***Consider listening style preferences.*** Interesting research shows that listening styles vary widely. For example, gender can affect listening style. When women listen, they tend to focus on the relationship. When they process information, their goal is to zoom in on emotions and mood. In an effort to relay support, women are typically willing to allow others to open up and reveal what they care about. By contrast, men tend to listen for facts and information and are less comfortable handling emotional content. They are typically interested in power and control, and they tend to listen for solutions rather than for empathy.[2]

   The *Guide to the Project Management Body of Knowledge* (*PMBOK® Guide—Sixth Edition*) recommends that a project manager should assess the communication styles of both speaker and listener in order to identify the preferred method, format, and content for formal interactions (section 10.1.2.6). After assessing, the manager will be able to tailor their listening behavior to the particular speaker more effectively.

5. ***Establish a range of listening channels.*** Different stakeholders may call for listening through different channels. For example, project managers know that they need to listen especially carefully to customers, a group of stakeholders that may be large and geographically dispersed. Many companies have teams that have developed technology to make it easier to actively listen to customers, and a handful of organizations have created a "chief listening officer" position. For instance, T-Mobile has established formal systems dedicated to listening to customers. CEO John Legere even had a phone line installed so he could listen to customer service calls. In 2018, he was named CEO of the year by GeekWire. In his award acceptance speech, Legere advised, "Listen to your employees. Listen to your customers…and do what they tell you."[3]

Other companies use social media as formal channels for listening to customers. Nike, for one, restructured its customer listening efforts in 2017, using platforms such as Twitter and Facebook to capture customers' opinions. But whether using state-of-the-art technology or simple face-to-face conversation, project managers must listen closely to all their stakeholders because the success of their project, and indeed their organization, requires adapting to their diverse needs.

Responding

Active listening not only involves receiving a message, it also calls for a response of some kind. When communicating formally with your project team members, customers, and other stakeholders, you are expected to receive and then respond to what they have said. An easy-to-remember formula for an effective response is ACE—Affirm, Comment, Expand.

Responding with the ACE Formula:

1. Affirm
2. Comment
3. Expand

Begin your response by *affirming* what you have heard the other person say. You accomplish this with a paraphrase, which reflects her meaning as you understood it rather than her exact words. After proving that you got the message, you can *comment* on it by saying whether you agree or disagree. Next you *expand* by explaining why you agree or disagree, adding your own two cents to the discussion.

Following the ACE formula will reduce defensiveness and encourage the team member to be receptive and open to your opinions and ideas.

Asking Questions

So far, we've examined one strategy for checking understanding—listening. A second strategy that will help you when you're trying to understand a message is to ask good questions. Jim Quigley, a former CEO at Deloitte, improved his communication style by talking no more than 20 percent of the time during meetings. Quigley explained, "One of my objectives is listening. Many times you can have bigger impact if you know what to ask, rather than knowing what to say." As he increased his questions, Quigley found himself gaining a deeper understanding of other people's needs.[4]

Project managers who ask questions not only improve their understanding, they also improve the relationship. Although people mostly talk about their own viewpoints during conversations, researchers at Harvard University found that asking for information from others makes one seem more responsive. And responsive people tend to be better liked.[5]

The type of answer you get will largely depend on the type of question you ask (see Table 3.1).

An *open-ended* question calls for a long answer. It is designed to open the door and get the other person talking. Typically it begins with "why," "what," "how," or "tell me about." You usually use open-ended questions at the beginning of a conversation.

A *closed-ended* question calls for a one-word answer such as a fact, a number, a date, a "yes" or "no." Typically it begins with "when," "how often," "how many," or "did you." You usually use closed-ended questions during a conversation to pin down information and seek commitment.

A *probe* is a secondary or follow-up question. It can be open or closed. When you want the speaker to elaborate, ask an open probe such as "And then what did she do?" When you want the speaker to provide clarification, ask a closed probe such as "How often has she done that?"

Table 3.1 Types of questions

Question type	Use	Example
Open	Get information Get the other person talking	What happened? What are you worried about?
Closed	Get commitment Get facts and details	Will you do that? When did that happen?
Probe	Get elaboration Get clarification	What happened after that? Was that before or after he called?
Directed	Get agreement	That was a mistake, wasn't it?

The Harvard researchers who identified a connection between asking questions and being liked also found that probes, in particular, are an important indicator of responsiveness. So if you ask a higher rate of follow-up questions, you will benefit in two ways—you will understand more, and you will strengthen your work relationship.

A *directed* question is a leading question. Typically, it begins with a statement and then calls for agreement. An example is, "You won't be late for work again, will you?" Use a directed question toward the end of a conversation, when you are seeking consensus.

Communicating Performance Expectations

This section focuses on strategies for making sure your team understands their roles and responsibilities to ensure project success. Once you are confident that everyone understands what is expected, your performance feedback becomes more pointed; later in the chapter you will discover strategies for responding if team members don't do what they are expected to do and forgiving corrective feedback. The chapter concludes by discussing conflict, offering five strategies for managing it.

Clarifying Goal Behaviors

If you've ever been surprised and disappointed when a team member said, "I don't know how to do that" or "I didn't know you wanted me to do that," this section is for you. Just because new members supposedly have the required job qualifications, there's no guarantee that they can hit the ground running. Rather than assuming they will step right in, it's important to take the time to communicate your expectations as clearly and completely as you can. That will not only reduce the members' performance anxiety, it will also build a trusting relationship and minimize the frequency of corrective performance feedback.

The Tell-Show-Do Formula. The classic model for teaching new team members how to do a job is "Tell-Show-Do" (Figure 3.1).

You may be interested to know that the Tell-Show-Do method was pioneered by an American educational psychologist named Robert Gagne, who had worked with the Army Air Corps during World War II

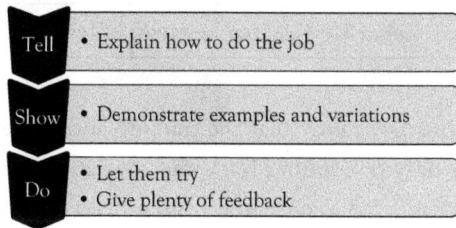

Figure 3.1 Training model

to train pilots. Since then, extensive research has validated Gagne's principles in educational and work settings.[6]

Formal Training Programs. If you want your team to do certain tasks and they aren't doing them correctly, don't jump to conclusions about their motivations, work attitudes, or intellect. First, check to be sure that they understand what you expect them to do. The following paragraphs will provide an overview of the training cycle, taking you through the process of determining what they know and don't know, designing and delivering formal training programs, and conducting follow-up evaluations.

Training Cycle:

1. Conduct a needs assessment
2. Design instructional materials
3. Determine logistics
4. Help adults learn
5. Evaluate outcomes

1. ***Conduct a needs assessment.*** The most obvious way to determine what someone already knows and doesn't know is to ask. But if you say, "Do you know how to do this?" they will usually say, "Yes, I do" out of fear that they will look incompetent.

    Instead, try an open-ended question like, "Tell me (or show me) how you do this." The gap between what they are doing and what you want them to do is the need for training. The goal of training is to close that gap between actual and optimal behaviors.

> Optimal behavior – Actual behavior = Training need

I will pause here to say that the training needs assessment (TNA) process not only determines important deviations from a standard. Project managers can also use the TNA process to anticipate changes in standards and prepare their teams to meet them. Thus, needs assessment can be proactive as well as reactive. Similarly, learning needs can be considered as an opportunity as well as a problem. In short, training facilitates change.

Of course, you can't solve every performance problem through training. Environmental barriers, conflicts between team members, equipment and supply issues, and cultural differences are just a few factors that you must consider when analyzing reasons for poor performance. But if your gap analysis shows that the need for training, the second step is to design an instructional program.

2. *Design instructional materials.* Most people are visual learners. That is, they remember what they see better than what they read or hear. In fact, listening is one of the poorest ways to learn for most people.

As Figure 3.2 shows, if your team members just listen, they will lose 90 percent of what you say after three days.[7] For maximum retention, you need to appeal to a combination of senses—give them something to look at, something to listen to, and something to read. Dreary lectures don't work well. The general rule of training is, get

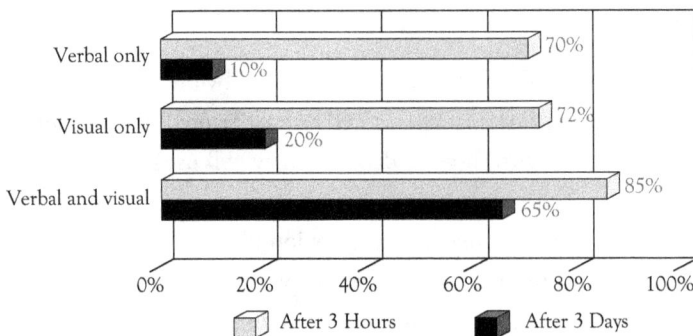

Figure 3.2 Percent of audience recall

learners to actively engage with the learning. And change things up every 20 minutes.

3. ***Determine logistics.*** Once you have determined the need for training and put together some materials, you must figure out when, where, and how the training will be delivered. Logistical issues can be daunting, so let's take them one at a time.

Many organizations have turned to computer-assisted delivery (CAD) in order to avoid logistical barriers. CAD programs are popular because they can be efficient and cost effective. Typically, employees sit at a computer and work through the training package at their own pace, and sometimes on their own time. Built-in measures of progress along the way can ensure that they don't just click through the material. Evidence of completion and test scores can be automatically reported back to the work unit and to human resources.

Face-to-face training classes, by comparison, are more time consuming and often more costly because of trainees' time away from work. Sessions are intensive but often more effective in terms of actual learning and facilitating behavior changes. Contract trainers can provide a fresh, unbiased viewpoint and a threat-free resource.

After deciding on the delivery format—CAD or face-to-face—you will have to select a training source. Often, your human resources office will help you find a vendor, either internal or external. Customized training is usually more costly than "off the shelf" prepackaged programs, but in the end it can be more effective because it is aimed at a narrower target of training needs.

4. ***Help adults learn***. Logistical issues are complex. Often you have to make do with an imperfect schedule, compromising on time, place, and length. But once you've nailed down those decisions, you can move on to considering how adults learn best.

A typical face-to-face training class should be organized like this.

How to Organize a Face-to-face Training Session:
Beginning

- Set goals
- Describe appropriate behaviors

- Explain methods
- Motivate participants to learn

Middle

- Broadcast structure of the program
- Balance lecture, discussion, practice, Q and A sessions
- Make learning fun, not frightening

End

- Review achievements
- Discuss transfer of learning to the work environment
- Suggest ways to reinforce the learning and overcome roadblocks
- Give rewards

Notice the level of trainee involvement in each segment. Adults learn best when they see the value of the learning. So in order to buy into the training, they must be able to connect the information with their own goals. They should be actively engaged every step of the way.

There are four learning styles, as identified in Figure 3.3: personal, analytical, practical, and innovative.[8] Becoming aware of the

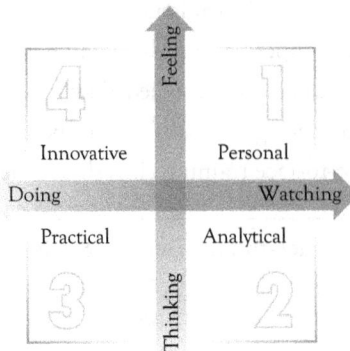

Figure 3.3 Learning styles

diversity of learning styles will make you a more culturally competent project manager.

In the next paragraphs, we will examine the four adult learning styles and consider training techniques to suit each.

The *Personal Learner* is high on feeling and watching. This style will relate material to their personal experience and do well discussing in groups, sharing their feelings, and interacting.

The *Analytical Learner* is high on thinking and watching. This style needs to know how facts relate to established knowledge and will do well in highly structured, systematic learning environments, lectures, and case studies.

The *Practical Learner* is high on doing and thinking. This style is results oriented and will do well in hands-on activities and simulations.

The *Innovative Learner* is high on doing and feeling. This style resists structure, enjoys considering possibilities, and flourishes when free to brainstorm and experiment.

Taking the time to identify your team members' preferred learning styles and developing training materials to suit them will pay off. Realize, however, that while it's not always practical or even possible, the best solution is to find a balance between nurturing and challenging (Figure 3.4). That is, try to build some elements into the training program that will maximize each learning style. For example, you could incorporate a group discussion for the personal learners, a brainstorming activity for the innovative learners, a case study for the analytical learners, and a simulation for the practical learners.

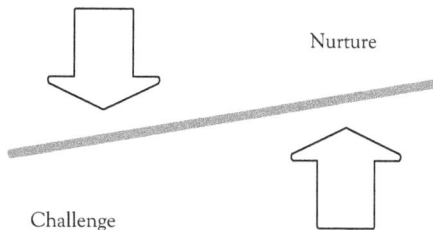

Figure 3.4 Balancing Act for facilitating learning

5. ***Evaluate outcomes.*** After the training program is completed, how can you be sure that it will stick? Donald Kirkpatrick, a top researcher in corporate training and development, identified four levels of evaluation and suggested that there are numerous ways to determine success.[9]

The first level of evaluation is the trainees' *reaction.* Immediately post-program, ask the trainees how they liked the training. Usually you can accomplish this with a satisfaction survey that asks for ratings of the instructor, the materials, the logistics, and the topics. Such a survey is generally referred to as a "smile sheet."

The second level of evaluation is trainee *learning.* Usually you can accomplish this with a test that you administer immediately post-program or after a short time has passed. Scores will indicate how much the trainees actually learned and remembered.

The third level of evaluation is trainee *behavior.* This is often the most important to project managers, because it measures whether the trainees can apply the new information back on the job. If this "transfer of training" does not occur, however, look for barriers other than trainee's ability. You may identify attitudinal and even environmental barriers to changing their behaviors.

The fourth level of evaluation is *results.* You can usually leave this level of evaluation to stakeholders such as human resources, finance, and operations executives who have access to data about your team's productivity and performance pre- and post-training. Identifying the elements that affect return on investment (ROI) can be slippery, since many factors other than the team's competence will influence performance.

Kirkpatrick's Levels of Training Evaluation:

1. Reaction
2. Learning
3. Behavior
4. Results

Giving Performance Feedback

After ensuring that you have clearly communicated expectations to the project team, your next step is to give continuous performance feedback, both positive and negative. It is easy to share information when it's neutral or positive. But giving negative feedback and bad news is tough. That's why many project managers delay or avoid it.

Giving Bad News to the Team

It's tough when you must give your team information they don't want to hear. Any change in policy or procedure is often unwelcome simply because it is a change. Generally, people are comfortable with the status quo, despite the tendency to complain about the way things are. When an impending change in policy or procedure will result in negative situations—reductions in compensation, relocation, increases in workload—it's even more important to announce the bad news without damaging the work relationship. The worst that can happen at this point is that the communication channels close up.

To keep the lines of communication open in bad times, follow these steps:

Format for a Bad News Message:

- Buffer
- Reasons
- Bad News
- Goodwill

---

1. **Begin with a buffer.** Typical buffers are a compliment ("Good job with that angry client yesterday, Ben"), statement of appreciation ("Thanks for taking my call"), agreement on a principle ("Safety is our top priority"), or a shared goal ("We've got to hit our deadline"). This establishes a positive, or at least neutral, connection.

2. ***Give reasons for the upcoming change.*** Presenting background information, facts and incidents, will help your team understand what's behind the decision.

3. ***Deliver the bad news.*** By now the team is prepared. They won't like what they hear, but they'll know why they are hearing it. Stick to the facts as you know them. Avoid sharing your doubts and other negative emotions, because feelings are contagious and they will take their cue from you.

4. ***End with goodwill.*** Express confidence in their ability to weather the change and reassure them that you'll remain at their side, supporting and keeping them informed throughout the transition.

Giving Corrective Feedback

Project managers need strategies for delivering negative feedback when a team member is performing inappropriately. For many reasons it's a mistake to avoid responding until the formal performance review. The time-honored formula for immediately correcting inappropriate behavior is DESC, which is based on the principles of behavioral psychology.

Steps for Corrective Feedback:

D = Describe
E = Express
S = Specify
C = Consequences

---

1. ***Describe*** the inappropriate behavior. It's important that you focus on behavior, or actions, rather than attitudes. For example, if you are dealing with a chronically tardy team member, describe the behavior concretely: "Jesse, you've shown up at least 10 minutes late for a meeting four times in the past two weeks." This sentence sticks to the facts.

   Don't confuse observations of behavior with assumptions about what's behind them. An observation or fact is something you can check. It is either true or false. An assumption is an opinion. It is neither true nor false, it's just an opinion. If you start talking to a team member about attitudes, such as, "Jesse, you're lazy and unreliable," you are going to have trouble defending your claims. Jesse is going to deny, deflect, and defend herself by responding with something like, "That's just your opinion." And she'll be right. That conversation is doomed.

2. *Express* why the behavior is inappropriate. This step is critical because you have to come up with a good reason for requiring a change in the behavior. If you can't justify the change, your team member is unlikely to put in the effort. Sometimes project managers will stoop to excuses like, "It's the policy" in an attempt to justify a required change, despite knowing how weak that sounds.

   The following true story will demonstrate the importance of step 2. Every morning a project manager set an alarm clock to go off loudly at 8:00 a.m. in the office to remind the team of the importance of promptness. They thought it was demeaning. When questioned about reasons that promptness was so important (other than that it was company policy), the project manager came up with a good explanation that had to do with being ready to pick up the phones when the customers started calling and placing orders. Once the project manager communicated this valid reason that tardiness was inappropriate, the team members' behaviors improved.

3. *Specify* the behavior you want the team members to adopt. Again, the emphasis here is on behaviors rather than attitudes. You must tell your team exactly what you want them to do. That should include how often, beginning when, and with what degree of accuracy.

4. Tell the *consequences* of adopting and not adopting the behavior. This step may seem obvious. Most companies have disciplinary procedures in place that human resources will gladly explain to you. Ensure that your team is well aware of organizational policies and procedures, along with the penalties for violations.

You may wonder why team members sometimes persist in doing what they know they shouldn't, such as coming in late or using office technology for non-work reasons. Behavioral psychologists have shown that behavior is shaped by a pattern of rewards. But what could possibly be a worker's reward for ignoring stated policy and coming to work late? Well, less time spent working, for one thing—that's a major reward for many people! And if there are no negative consequences that counteract the reward, the worker will be motivated to do it again. Other possible rewards for inappropriate behaviors include getting attention, retribution for perceived slights, and an enhanced self-image for defying authority. Simply put, if you want a behavior to stop, figure out the reward and withhold it.

But what about the other part of step 4—telling the consequences for correcting a behavior? "Oh, that's easy," you may say. "If the team member adopts the behaviors I expect, they get to keep their positions." True, but is that enough motivation? Often it isn't. Continuous positive reinforcement such as personal statements of recognition ("I noticed how hard you've been working on the project this week") or appreciation ("Thanks for getting those numbers to me ahead of schedule") are more powerful ways to reward and maintain expected behaviors.

> Reward team members when they do something right.
> Don't reward them when they do something wrong.

As you will read in Chapter 4, positive interpersonal relationships between project managers and their teams are powerful motivators. Can you say "thank you" too often? Probably not. These simple words make people feel valued.

Conducting Formal Performance Reviews

Periodically, you may be called on to conduct formal performance reviews of your team members. While the benefits of formal performance reviews seem obvious, in fact many managers conduct them ineffectively and reluctantly because they do not like to be put into the role of evaluator. Some may fear that the discomfort created by a poorly conducted performance review will destroy their working relationship with the team.

Remember that there should be no surprises in a performance review. If you've dealt with negative behaviors on the spot and rewarded positive behaviors as you caught them, and if your relationship with your team is open and honest, then all of you will already know what to expect during a formal evaluation session.

The following information will help your performance reviews have better outcomes.

Preparation Steps for Performance Reviews:

1. Purpose
2. Timing
3. Location
4. Content
5. Outcome

Purpose. Typically, performance reviews (1) focus on past performance, or (2) focus on future performance, including goal setting that leads to improvement. The ideal review will cover both purposes, plus two more: (3) focus on the team leader's past performance, and (4) focus on the team leader's future performance, including goal setting. Thus, a formal opportunity for two-way feedback about the past and the future will benefit both parties.

Timing. Formal reviews are most often conducted once a year, with the understanding that the project manager's feedback should be given to team members whenever needed. There should be no surprises during a formal review because it should be a summary of prior conversations including positive feedback, corrective feedback, career path, and compensation.

Why perform a formal review once a year when you provide regular, frequent feedback? Periodic "course correction" makes sense for even very satisfactory team members. Also, certain situations, such as the completion of a major project or unusually poor performance, require a formal session. Consider the entire situation when determining the best time for a formal performance interview.

Once you've selected the time, tell the team well in advance so they can prepare psychologically. Avoid the "stop by my desk as soon as you get a chance" type of announcement.

Location. Once the purpose and timing are set, consider the best place for the interview. Often, the best place for the interview is a neutral, safe, private space that maximizes two-way interaction.

Message Content. Next, focus on the content of the session. Regardless of the specific purpose, review the dimensions of the team member's assignments, review notes from the previous performance review and recent occurrences. You may even want to ask other team members and other stakeholders for their feedback. After gathering all your feedback documents, list specific items you want to cover in the performance review interview.

During the interview, the more you let the team member talk, the more likely that open and valuable communication will result. Studies show that managers who encourage a self-review of performance are more satisfying than those based strictly on manager-prepared appraisals.[10] For useful feedback in both directions and reasonable goal setting, you must establish trust through two-way communication.

Begin the performance review with positive feedback and ask the team member open questions such as, "What accomplishments are you most proud of this year?" This tactic helps to establish a supportive climate and two-way interaction. Once aware that you do appreciate past success, the team member is likely to be more receptive to corrective feedback.[11]

Outcome. At the end of the performance review, be sure that you both compose action plans for improvement. Contribute to each other's action plans and agree on them. They should be behavior-based, specific, concrete, achievable, and challenging. To show seriousness of intent, you might each sign them. These action plans may be in addition to any employee appraisal forms that your human resources department expects you to complete. The key is to create a perception of a common goal that you both will work toward.

Action Plan Contents:

- What I will do
- When I will do it

- With whom I will do it
- What I expect to be the result
- How I will know I am successful

Giving Performance Feedback to Culturally Diverse Workers

Formal performance appraisals are unique to U.S. work environments. In many other countries, especially collectivist and high power distance cultures, the assumption is that workers will always give 100 percent. This attitude may be grounded in the fact that a single family often controls an entire industry, so when you work for family, you continually give your best effort to make the business profitable and the family prosperous. Deep involvement and commitment make feedback from managers unnecessary.

A more complex situation occurs when workers in a U.S. business come from one of these other cultures. For example, in a manufacturing company that was one of my clients, the laborers were predominantly Vietnamese, while the production managers and supervisors were Anglo-American and Hispanic. The managers had difficulty getting their workers to take direction; they typically ignored both positive and negative feedback, sitting passively during formal performance reviews. Close observation revealed that the workers listened only to their Vietnamese elders on the shop floor. From then on, the managers simply communicated to the elders what they wanted from the workers, and the elders made sure it happened.

Managing Conflict

Continuing our examination of tough formal communication challenges that project managers face, this chapter ends with a look at conflict and five strategies for managing clashes between the manager and the team, sponsors, and other stakeholders.

Tensions can run high at work. As a project manager, you are likely to spend up to 35 percent of your time dealing with complaints and handling disruptions in your fast-paced, diverse work environment.[12] When is conflict beneficial and when is it harmful?

Pros and Cons of Workplace Conflict

Conflict generally is considered a negative influence that is destructive; however, it can be a positive influence if you manage it properly. Conflict forces you to analyze goals, it creates dialogue among team members, and it fosters creative solutions. It has been linked to organizational learning, and even to improved performance and productivity. Without conflict, employees and organizations would stagnate.

Conflict between diverse age groups is one example of how conflict can be positive. For the first time in U.S. history, four generations are working together. Conflict commonly is due to differences in their work style and philosophy. Older workers typically view "work" as a place—a location you go to at a specified time, such as 9 a.m. to 5 p.m. Younger workers tend to view "work" as something you do—anywhere, any time. They grew up in a digital world where information is always available. So it's easy for Boomers to conclude that Millennials who arrive at 9:30 are working less hard than they, who arrived at 8:30, not realizing that the younger generation may have already put in time at their home computers or smartphones while still in pajamas. To Millennials, rigid scheduling of work is unnecessary. Boomers can benefit from their younger coworkers by learning that much of today's work can be done in flextime for maximum efficiency.

Conflict also may foster creativity. Conflict helps to overcome biases by forcing you out of your traditional ways of thinking. In this way, conflict promotes the unstructured thinking that lets you develop good, novel alternatives to difficult problems.[13]

Perhaps most importantly, decisions are better when there is open opposition and resistance. In one study, high-quality decisions occurred in 46 percent of the situations with strong worker resistance, but in only 19 percent of the situations where resistance was weak or non-existent.[14] Thus, if you are a manager who prides yourself on running a smooth ship, you may not be as effective as you think. The smooth ship may reflect suppressed conflict that could have potential benefit if allowed free play. In fact, the conflict might not be as harmful as suppressing it is.

Benefits of Conflict:

- Forces goal analysis
- Creates dialogue among employees
- Fosters creative solutions
- Stimulates organizational learning
- Improves performance and productivity
- Prevents stagnation

Strategies for Managing Conflict

Once you have pinpointed the sources of workplace conflict, you are ready to manage the conflict. This section offers five strategies for managing conflict; keep in mind that different conflict situations call for different strategies, so effective communication means that you match the strategy to the situation.

Avoid. You might think that the best way to handle conflict is to avoid it. The avoidance or withdrawal strategy combines a low concern for production with a low concern for people. If you use this style a lot, you see conflict as useless. Rather than undergo the tension and frustration of conflict, you use avoidance simply to remove yourself from conflict situations, either physically or psychologically. You dislike tension, don't take sides in a disagreement among others, and feel little commitment to any decisions reached. This conflict management style is the second most popular among U.S. managers.

Avoidance doesn't need to be dramatic. You can avoid by ignoring a hurtful comment or quickly changing the subject when conversation begins to threaten. Another way to avoid is to place the responsibility for an issue onto someone else. A third way to withdraw is to use a simple response of "I'm looking into the matter," with the hopes that the issue will be forgotten.

The avoidance strategy is frequently used in large bureaucracies that have too many policies. Rather than tackling the conflict, you simply blame it on "policy." If you lack self-confidence in your communication abilities, you may hope the problem just disappears. However, following the dictum, "never complain, never explain," usually doesn't work in the long run. In fact, withdrawal has been negatively associated with knowledge of others' feelings and attitudes, perceived helpfulness of the team, and strength of the planning relationship. Thus, avoiding conflict doesn't usually make things better in critical managerial areas.[15]

Accommodate. The second type of conflict resolution is accommodating. You try to deal with conflict by giving in, hoping to make everyone happy. When using this approach, you emphasize maintaining relationships with others, and you de-emphasize achieving productive goals. Since you are aiming for goodwill, you often give in to others' desires because you believe confrontation is always destructive.

Typical attempts to accommodate may include such things as calling for a coffee break at a tense moment, breaking tension by cracking a joke, saying "you're right" when they're not, or engaging in some ritual show of togetherness such as an office birthday party. Since these efforts are likely to reduce feelings of conflict, they are better than simple avoidance. But handling conflict by giving in probably will have short-range effects. Just because someone does not experience a hostile or negative feeling does not mean the real cause of the conflict is resolved. In fact, accommodating is a camouflage approach that can break down at any time and create barriers to progress.

In addition, accommodating hurts open communication and participation in goal setting. Think of your latest performance review. Did you give in to the judgments of your work quality without discussion or pushback? If so, did the reviewer think you had accepted the judgments as fair and true? How did you feel afterward—motivated to work harder? Probably not.

Compromise. Compromise, the third strategy for conflict resolution, assumes that half a loaf is better than none. Since compromise provides some gain for both sides rather than a unilateral victory or loss, you might judge this approach to be better than the strategies previously described.

Compromise is used when one of two conditions exists: (1) neither person thinks he/she can force their way on the other person, or (2) one or both people believes winning may not be worth the cost in money, time, or energy. Compromise is often highly related to negotiating, which is a legitimate conflict resolution strategy in today's workplace. Compromising may make both parties think they won, but they may also both feel like losers. The working relationship may become negative and distrustful.

A second concern with compromise is that the person with the most information has the better position, usually the person who has a better network. This power of information may restrict open communication, often resulting in a lopsided compromise. A third factor is the principle of the least-interested party: The party that has the least interest in the outcome is the more powerful person in the negotiations. As a result, a team member who has little concern about your welfare or the team's welfare may have the most influence in a compromise.

Force. Project managers often use force when they need to meet deadlines and goals at all costs, without concern for the needs or feelings of the team. Not surprisingly, forcing is the favorite conflict resolution strategy of U.S. managers. The forcing strategy will probably cause later conflicts, however, and can result in long-lasting emotional wounds.

The long-term effects will probably also include a loss of productivity. Forcing in conflict situations is negatively associated with adequacy of planning, helpfulness of the supervision, and participation in goal setting. The major result of forcing is that your team may become reluctant to carry out directives because they think that the ultimate resolution of the conflict will put them on the losing side of a win–lose position.

Clearly, forcing has limited use. Project managers should consider forcing to be a backup strategy for dealing with conflict only when immediate compliance is called for but not as a long-term solution.

Collaborate. The fifth strategy is a win–win. This complex and highly effective style requires skillful, strategic managerial communication, but it reaps a big dividend. The key to this strategy is that it follows a mutual problem-solving approach rather than a combative one. Project managers who collaborate assume that a high quality, mutually acceptable solution is possible. Everyone directs energies toward defeating the problem and not each other.

Steps in the Collaboration Process:

1. Define the problem
2. Analyze the problem
3. Brainstorm solutions
4. Develop criteria for a good solution
5. Find the best match
6. Follow up

Here are the six steps in the collaboration process:

1. **Define the problem.** The problem definition must be specific. Stating the problem in a conflict situation is usually much more difficult than it seems, and most people jump to solutions before they clearly define the problem. Because of this, our inclination is to state the problem as a solution rather than as a goal, which results in ambiguous communication. The outcome may be increased conflict. One helpful strategy is to write out the problem statement clearly, so everyone can see it and agree on it. Or you can agree on a problem stated as a question. State goals in the form of team goals rather than your own goals.

2. **Analyze the problem.** Again, most people want to skip this step. After all, they may argue, they live with the problem. What is the point of spending more time wallowing in it? The answer is that by exploring the depths of the problem, by looking at its history, causes, effects, and extent, you can later come up with a solution that addresses more than symptoms, one that is more than a bandage. This analysis step will uncover the root cause of the problem, thus improving the chances of being successful.

3. **Brainstorm alternatives.** Everyone involved in the conflict should offer potential solutions. One idea may stimulate other ideas. The more you communicate in an open, trusting environment, the greater the potential for finding effective solutions. Trust, of course, evaporates when an idea is criticized during a brainstorming session.

As soon as someone says, "That's a terrible idea. It'll never work," who would be willing to take the risk of coming up with another idea? Make sure that you don't judge ideas prematurely.

4. **Develop criteria for a good solution.** These criteria, or standards, may already be in place and available. Occasionally, you and your team are allowed to develop your own criteria. It is important to delay developing the list of criteria until after step 3, brainstorming, has been completed. Otherwise, the identification of alternatives could be stymied by the group's preconceived evaluations.

    The most common criteria for a good solution are:
    - It must be cheap
    - It must be easy to do
    - It must tap resources already on hand
    - It must be legal
    - It must align with the organization's mission or values

5. **Evaluate the brainstormed alternatives using the criteria.** This is really the easiest step. By now, you have reached agreement on the problem, and everyone has had a say about possible solutions. The best solution will appear naturally because it is the brainstormed alternative that matches your list of criteria.

6. **Follow up.** You never really know that you have solved the problem unless you follow up after the solution has been implemented to be sure it meets the defined criteria. Checking to see how well the solution is working, and shoring it up when it falters, will lead to continuous process improvement.

You might be asking, if collaborating is the best all-around strategy for resolving conflict, why don't we do it more often? The simple answer is that this process calls for two prerequisites: time and ability. You can't count on reaching consensus on a solution right away. Hearing everyone out takes time and patience, commodities that are rare in today's workplace. Secondly, the team must already know how to collaborate; they must be familiar with, and be willing to follow, the six steps described previously.

Table 3.2 summarizes when each strategy works best and the result that project managers can expect.

Table 3.2 When to use each conflict resolution strategy

Conflict resolution strategy	When it works best	Result
Avoiding	• There's little chance you'll get your way • The potential damage of addressing the conflict outweighs the benefits of resolution • People need a chance to cool down • Others are in a better position to resolve the conflict • The problem will go away by itself	I lose You lose
Accommo-dating	• Preserving harmony is important • Personal antagonism is the major source of conflict • The issue itself is unsolvable • You care more about the relationship than getting your way	I lose You win
Compromising	• Two opponents are equal in power • Temporary settlements on complex issues are needed • Opponents do not share goals • Forcing or problem solving won't work	I half win, half lose You half win, half lose
Forcing	• Quick, decisive action is needed, as in a crisis • A rule has to be enforced • You know you're right • You must protect yourself	I win You lose
Collaborating	• Both sets of concerns are too important to be compromised • It is important to work through hard feelings • Commitment to the resolution is important • A permanent solution is desired	I win You win

Summary

This chapter describes formal interpersonal communication situations that project managers engage in and provides practical strategies, techniques, and methods that will ensure the success of the interaction. It begins by examining the importance of managers' ability to receive information effectively. Three strategies that managers should use are listening, responding, and asking questions. Next the chapter explains how project managers can ensure that their team understands what is expected of them.

Strategies that managers should use to communicate expectations are the Tell-Show-Do formula and formal training programs. The third section of this chapter focuses on the importance of giving regular performance feedback. Managers should give both positive and negative feedback on a regular basis as well as during formal performance review sessions to ensure continued high performance of their team. The chapter concludes with a look at conflict, explaining why it should be managed rather than discouraged, and presenting five strategies for managing conflict.

Questions

1. Which principles of effective listening described in this chapter are the most important for your project team to improve? How will you help your team to develop those listening competencies?

2. Analyze a past formal performance review interview that you conducted, using the principles outlined in this chapter. What should you have done differently?

3. Identify one element in your project team that causes destructive conflict and one element that causes constructive conflict. How can you manage each?

4. Which of the six steps in the collaboration process that is outlined in this chapter is the most challenging for your project team? How will you overcome the challenges?

CHAPTER 4

Informal Interpersonal Communication

Chapter Objectives

The purpose of this chapter is to help project managers learn strategies and techniques for key interpersonal communication competencies that can be applied in informal settings:

- Developing trust
- Developing emotional intelligence
- Increasing employee engagement
- Building rapport

As discussed in Chapter 3, the formal interpersonal communication that you engage in upward, downward, laterally, and diagonally along the organizational hierarchy will to a great extent determine your project's success. Furthermore, the Sequence for Success model introduced in Chapter 1 (Figure 4.1) shows that interpersonal communication is the first step in the sequence model, culminating in your organization's success. That's because communication leads to relationships; relationships foster important emotional conditions such as loyalty, job satisfaction, and commitment; and in turn, these emotional conditions trigger effective work performance. The more people engage in an organization's life, the more connected they become and the more effective the organization becomes.

This chapter builds on the communication competencies discussed in the previous chapter, those that are useful in formal professional settings. We now focus on the daily informal conversations that will help you get along with your project team, sponsors, and stakeholders. The chapter describes a range of communication strategies that will build stronger

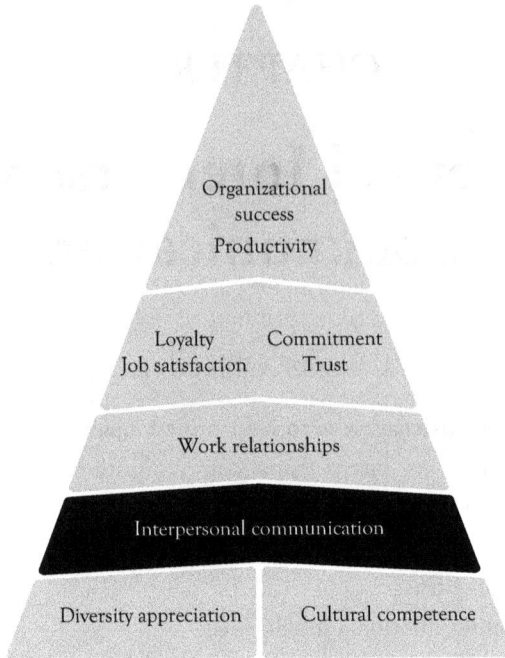

Figure 4.1 Communication and the sequence for success

work relationships. The relationship level is where most of the work gets done. It's also where you experience most of the difficulties.

Trust

Establishing trust is an important responsibility of a project manager. A project manager can build trust among the team members informally every day as they work together, share problems and find solutions, collaborate to make decisions, and handle conflicts. Routine meetings and informal conversations are opportunities to develop trust between the project manager and all stakeholders.

Why is developing trust important? First, trust is the key for successful collaboration and cooperation among team members. Further, trust enables managers to motivate stakeholders to achieve a project's goals. Putting your people first, helping them to feel engaged and committed, is a matter of trust above all else. Today's workers look for a place where they can do their best work. They look for cultural fit and trusting relationships on the job.

> Openness and transparency in communication instill trust among the project team members.

Trusting Them

If you want your project team to trust you, then you must trust them. Here's the extent to which Sharon Sloane, CEO of Will Interactive, trusts her people:

> We give what we call mission-type orders here. I will be very clear with what the goal is, what the objective is. Then I'm basically going to give you the latitude to do it. If you need my help or have a problem, come see me. Otherwise, I bless you.[1]

Trusting your team means nurturing their independence, allowing them the freedom to express their opinions and follow preferred work styles without denying those of others. This willingness to let people approach the work their preferred way—so long as the goal is achieved—is particularly important if you have a culturally diverse workforce. Diverse environments call for a high tolerance for disagreement. Ask yourself, "Which is more important—that things get done my way, or that things get done?"

A healthy work climate is a trusting climate. Douglas McGregor, a famous expert in organizational communication, summarized the optimal characteristics of a work climate:

1. The atmosphere is informal, relaxed, and comfortable.
2. Everyone participates in discussion about the work at hand.
3. Everyone is committed to the task and the objective.
4. Everyone listens to each other. Every idea is given a fair hearing.
5. Disagreement is not suppressed. Rather than silencing dissent, the reasons are examined, and the group seeks rational solutions.
6. Important decisions are reached by consensus.
7. Criticism is frequent, frank, and relatively comfortable, but not personal.
8. People freely express their feelings.

9. The leader does not dominate.

10. The group monitors itself.[2]

Do these characteristics sound like the characteristics of your project team? If you are comfortable hearing differences expressed, if you trust people to find their own way to reach the project's goals, the result will be relational satisfaction, commitment to excellence, and organizational success.

Trusting You

Of course, if you want your project team to trust you, you need to be trustworthy, yourself. The following paragraphs present ways to develop trust. Briefly, trust is developed when your words, nonverbals, and actions are *consistent*; your behaviors are *predictable*; and you explain what is going on and why (*transparency*).

Elements of Trust:

- Consistency
- Predictability
- Transparency

Let's take a closer look at these factors. First, make your words consistent with your nonverbal behaviors and actions. When what you say is inconsistent with how you act, look and sound, people believe how you look and sound. For instance, if you say, "These procedural changes are going to be an improvement," while looking glum and acting despondent, your team won't believe the changes will be beneficial, and they will resist adopting them.

Appropriate *nonverbal* behaviors for managers can be summarized as those demonstrating a confident manner. Confidence builds trust. Stand and sit straight, keep your head balanced on your neck, and be aware of eye contact patterns. Use a clear, pleasant but strong tone of voice and minimize disfluencies ("uh," "um," "you know," "like").

Appropriate *verbal* behaviors for managers who want to build trust include using inclusive words such as "we," "us," and "our" rather than "I" and "my." In this way the project manager signals a social category that will increase loyalty and trust for team members. Another verbal tool is to disclose more frequently, sharing information as much and as often as you can. This will reduce uncertainty and increase trust, even if your stakeholders won't like what they hear. Telling people more about what's going on will also increase predictability. A third verbal tool is to use concrete language—facts and words with clear meanings—rather than abstract or vague terms. Speaking conceptually or with lofty, vague expressions causes doubt and distrust.

Trustworthy talk is

- Inclusive
- Frequent
- Complete
- Concrete
- Honest

Finally, trustworthy talk is honest. The 2012 Edelman Trust Barometer calls for companies to "practice radical transparency," which means telling employees the truth about what's going on.[3] If an organization routinely shares information, stakeholders feel a sense of belonging and a part of a shared mission. This develops a bond of trust among everyone affiliated with the organization. Leaders who are transparent, who openly share truthful information, retain credibility.

Trust and External Stakeholders

As projects progress, managers should apply the principles in this section not only to their teams but also to external stakeholders, such as sponsors and customers. Remembering that the most important success factor in projects is customer satisfaction, wise project managers try especially hard to keep their customers informed throughout the project. Whether using formal progress reports or informal conversations, frequent communication with external stakeholders will help to develop a trusting relationship. The strength of this relationship may be tested when problems arise and bad news needs to be conveyed. At such times, open and honest communication of information will help keep everyone onboard. Further, frank discussion of problems with stakeholders may help to adjust expectations and even uncover solutions. Developing and maintaining stakeholder trust is a key for project success.

Emotional Intelligence

In addition to the ability to develop trusting relationships, a second crucial interpersonal competency for project managers is emotional intelligence (EI). This section defines this competency, explains why it is crucial, and shows you how to develop it.

How good are you at staying calm under pressure at work? When a team member complains to you, do you show empathy even though deep down you may feel that they are just whining? Does your project team think you are easy to get along with? Is it easy to socialize with your team?

Such behaviors reflect social and emotional competence. Popularly known as EI, social and emotional competence has been shown to be a better predictor of professional success than cognitive intelligence or specialized knowledge.[4] In fact, research shows that EI accounts for an amazing 58 percent of performance in all job types. Furthermore, 90 percent of high job performers are also high in EI, yet only 20 percent of low job performers are high in EI.

> *Emotional Intelligence* is the ability to recognize, understand, and respond to emotions in ourselves and others.

Research focusing on business leaders shows that EI scores are the highest for middle managers but lowest for executives. In trying to explain that difference, the researchers observed that executives are more likely to be promoted because of what they know or how long they have worked, rather than for their management skills or social awareness. However, high EI executives are the best performers.[5]

Unlike personality, which remains stable throughout most of our lives, EI can be improved with training. By improving our ability to recognize and understand emotions, we can do a much better job of managing our behavior and our social interactions. Daniel Goleman's landmark book about EI lists six ways people can cope with workplace pressures and the resulting stress on relationships. These competencies are generally accepted as the starting point for emotion management. They include the ability to

- Become self-aware in managing emotions and controlling impulses
- Set goals and perform well
- Be motivated and creative
- Empathize with others
- Handle relationships effectively
- Develop appropriate social skills[6]

Mastering these competencies will greatly affect the way you interact with team members, sponsors, and other stakeholders.

In their book, *Emotional Intelligence 2.0*, Bradberry and Greaves offer many practical suggestions for improving your self-awareness, managing yourself, becoming more socially aware, and managing workplace relationships. Here are some highlights that apply to project leaders:

- During meetings, use people's names. Don't take too many notes, but use nonverbal behaviors (looking, nodding) to indicate that you are paying attention as you listen.
- When interacting with culturally diverse people, be open, be respectful, be sincere, and be curious.
- During disagreements, acknowledge the other person's point or feelings before stating your own opinion. Be willing to offer a "fix it" statement no matter who is right.
- When interacting with your team, use compliments liberally, and always be pleasant and courteous.
- Have tough conversations instead of letting problems fester.

- When things explode, under-react until you have learned more.
- Get real value out of every social interaction, even with people you don't like.

EI and the Grapevine

Chapter 3 described the importance of listening when a project manager is engaged in formal communication situations. But informal, casual listening can also be extremely important for building your EI. As a project manager, you should always be aware of the rumors that circulate on the grapevine. At times, these rumors can provide important information; at other times, it may be important to change the rumors; and sometimes it's best to ignore the rumors. But always stay tuned in.

What causes rumors in project teams? To answer this question, the following formula is helpful:

$$Rumors = Ambiguity \times Interest$$

Rumors are created when the situation is ambiguous. If all information were available and clear from the formal channels, no rumors would be created. When the situation is ambiguous and also interesting, rumors will fly. This relationship has an important implication for project managers. By paying attention to the grapevine, you can determine what is interesting to your team.

Research indicates that information on the grapevine in organizations is 70 to 90 percent accurate. However, some amount of distortion always exists.[7] This core of truth along with the degree of distortion is often what makes a message on the grapevine believable, interesting, and durable.

As information moves from person to person on the grapevine, it tends to undergo three kinds of change. The first change is *leveling*, where details are dropped or simplified. This process is especially prevalent when the rumor is extremely complex. The second kind of change is *sharpening*, where people add drama and vivid details. People try to make a story better and more entertaining as they pass it along. The third change is *assimilating,* the tendency of people to adjust or modify rumors, to mold them to fit their personal needs. This makes the rumor more useful to those feeding the grapevine.

How Information Changes as it Moves through the Grapevine:

- Leveling
- Sharpening
- Assimilating

If you are a high EI manager, as you listen to informal communication, you try to determine the extent to which leveling, sharpening, and assimilation have occurred. Inaccurate rumors can sometimes call for action. Let's say your project team is working to introduce new machinery in a manufacturing environment, and rumors are flying about a massive layoff because of the new machinery being installed. If you hear these incorrect rumors, you can't ignore them. Members of the team should meet formally with employees to assure them no layoffs will occur and that the new equipment will offer significant benefits. Listening to rumors will help you to prevent losses in employee morale. As one manager once said to me, "It's important to listen to the talk on the street."

People prefer to get their information from formal (official, organization-sponsored) channels, but they turn to informal channels (the grapevine) when the formal channels have dried up because no one can work in a vacuum. Project managers with high EI will keep in mind the relationship between formal and informal communication channels.

EI and Daily Interactions with the Team

What are some ways that high EI managers communicate with their teams on a daily, informal basis? Project management experts Kathryn Wells and Tim Kloppenborg recommend that team interactions should be characterized by the behaviors shown in Table 4.1.[8]

Table 4.1 Checklist for high EI communication

Communicate openly and honestly
Investigate to find the truth, then communicate it
Admit and learn from your mistakes
Treat everyone fairly
Speak calmly
Make requests instead of demands
Don't complain about what cannot be changed
Acknowledge when something is done well
Handle negative situations in a positive manner

These techniques are not simple or easy to adopt, but project managers will find that they are worth working on, for they are powerful tools to enhance the effectiveness of informal communication with the team.

Case Example of Emotional Intelligence. Let's apply some of these EI behaviors to a hypothetical case. You are the manager of a project team that has been tasked to investigate health benefits packages and recommend one for the organization's employees. The team consists of department heads as well as subject matter experts (SMEs) from Human Resources. Lately you've seen a drop in the Accounting Department head's attendance at meetings and a couple of missed deadlines. She has even started ignoring your e-mails. You're concerned about the team member's commitment and willingness to carve out time for the project. What should you do?

Because you are a high EI project manager you understand that the team member probably considers the project to be "more work," and nothing else. As such, project tasks are being pushed down to the bottom of her priority list. In a private informal conversation with the member, preferably face to face, you begin by acknowledging that other commitments are probably interfering with her ability to complete the project assignments. Next, you explore possibilities for adjusting the project's timelines to fit her calendar. Perhaps you could schedule meetings for a different time, place, or day of the week, thereby showing flexibility.

A related issue is the efficiency of your meetings. If you suspect that's the problem, you admit that meeting management is a competency you are working on, and you invite her suggestions for ensuring that the meetings are never a waste of the team members' precious time.

Toward the end of the conversation, you ask the department head to describe her professional goals, searching for ways that the project could help her achieve some of these goals. Money, recognition, promotion, and résumé building are some possibilities to explore. By aligning the department head's goals with the project's goals and the organization's goals, you encourage her participation in the project and improve performance. You also strengthen your work relationship by demonstrating empathy, which will reap important rewards.

Engagement

Let's look again at the Sequence for Success model described in Chapter 1, focusing on the fourth level, the building block that captures key emotional conditions caused by strong work relationships—"loyalty, commitment, job satisfaction, and trust" (Figure 4.2). You may ask, "Why should I worry about such emotions? I have to work with this project team, but I don't have to like them." True. In fact, if you ever find project stakeholders that you like well enough to become friends outside of work, that's a bonus. More often, however, the people we consider to be our friends will disappear from our lives when they (or we) leave the project or organization.

On the other hand, a strong case can be made for trying to develop positive relationships with your team so that these key emotions—loyalty, commitment, and satisfaction—occur. These emotions are manifested in engagement.

Engagement means that your team will:

- Identify with the project's goals and values
- Want to belong to the team
- Be willing to display effort on behalf of the team

Research consistently shows that low engagement leads to absenteeism, turnover, and unrest. On the other hand, high engagement leads to trust, quality and quantity of communication, involvement, and

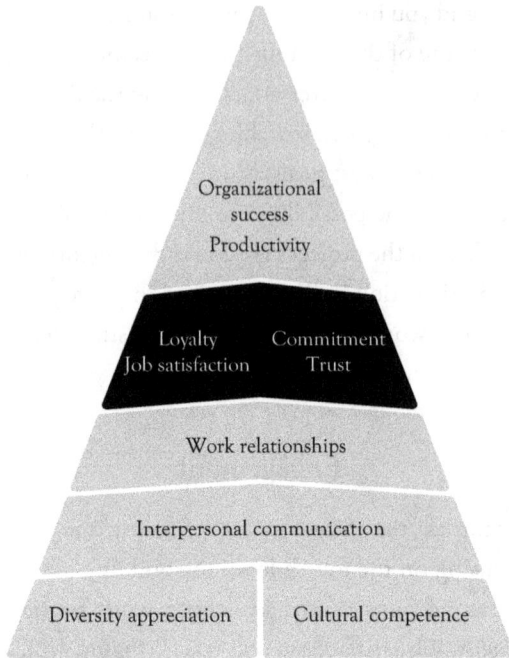

Figure 4.2 Key emotional conditions and the sequence for success

productivity. Therefore, if you treat your team well, they will work harder for you. The connection between job performance and key emotions is well established. When employees feel a sense of loyalty, commitment, job satisfaction, and trust, their productivity improves, so that the project and, ultimately, the organization can succeed.

> The most crucial success factor in project management is effective communication.

Impact of Engagement

Employee engagement is a hot topic. Engaged workers are committed, involved, enthusiastic, and energized. Engaged workers typically are also high performers. Alarmingly, however, a 2013 Gallup survey showed that only 30 percent of U.S. employees describe themselves as engaged at work. Around the world, across 142 countries, the proportion of engaged employees drops to 13 percent. When asked why, the workers complained about the lack of opportunity for self-expression, personal growth, and meaningful work. In short, most felt dissatisfied and discouraged.[9]

Engagement levels appear to be particularly weak among Millennials. In a 2011 Harris Interactive report commissioned by the Career Advisory Board, "meaning" was the top career priority for those between the ages of 21 and 31. If you are from a previous generation, you are more likely to value loyalty to the company above meaningful work. You may even be willing to admit that you've complained about younger employees' lack of commitment to their organization. But it's risky for managers to ignore such generational differences in priorities, whether real or imagined, because they may affect morale, retention, and even productivity.

> Engaged teams are committed, involved, enthusiastic, energized, and productive.

In the face of such overwhelming research findings, we must acknowledge that the way people feel at work profoundly influences how they perform. Managers who think that pay is the primary influence on performance haven't been paying attention. Although financial rewards are relevant—who among us would work for free?—the psychological and emotional rewards are what keep us on the job.

What drives engagement? In a word, communication. The Great Place To Work Institute found that employees enjoy working in an environment where they "trust the people they work for, have pride in what they do and enjoy the people they work with."[10] Such positive work environments are typically characterized by open communication.

While larger companies may expect formal channels maintained by their Communication Department to broadcast information internally and externally, most project teams consider their managers to be the most important source of transparency. As a project manager, you are expected to informally share relevant information with subordinates; you are responsible for promoting a sense of belonging and commitment, and helping your team to understand the mission. These behaviors develop trust, which leads to employee engagement.

Facilitating Team Engagement

Project managers can take some simple steps to foster informal communication (see Table 4.2). To increase social communication, try introducing shared coffee breaks each day and shared birthday celebrations each month. Replace individual coffee makers scattered around the workspace with a large cafe area. Remove small tables and provide larger ones in the cafeteria to facilitate more interaction.

Table 4.2 Ways to foster engagement

Institute shared coffee breaks and celebrations
Provide environments for socializing
Encourage sharing information and helping
Discourage reliance on technology
Conduct retention surveys and act on the results

An example presented in Chapter 1 illustrates another strategy for fostering engagement. A study of engineers at a San Francisco telecommunications firm who shared the most information and gave the most help to colleagues were found to be the most productive and were held in the highest respect by their peers. Furthermore, the most helpful engineers built up more trust and attracted more cooperation from across their work groups, as well as from the people they helped.[11]

A fourth way to facilitate engagement, as shown in Table 4.2, is to discourage habitual use of technology for routine interactions. The single best tool to enhance engagement is face-to-face, one-to-one communication. As a manager, you can increase your teams' level of engagement by talking to them more often than e-mailing or messaging them. Being present allows you to notice and acknowledge their contributions more often. Stop by and ask whether they had a good day and what moments made it so. Then listen. Try to adjust the work environment to make those moments happen more frequently. Encourage others to do the same.

A final suggestion to keep your team happy is to find out why they stay. Conducting an exit survey may reveal the working conditions—or people—that drove someone away, but it's too late at that point to impact the leaver's attitudes. Instead, consider conducting a retention survey among current team members. A retention survey can make people feel valued and will determine what the organization can do to improve member satisfaction, whether it's training, benefits, improved communication channels, or recognition programs. You might even consider asking retention survey-type questions during annual performance reviews. A team member's responses might trigger redesigning the individual's job to make it more closely align with personal strengths and passions.

> An engaged workforce is a happier workforce and a more productive workforce.

Facilitating Organizational Engagement

Engagement is important on a macro level as well as on the team level. When team members feel a strong emotional bond to their employer organization, they will recommend it to others and commit time and effort to help the organization succeed.

For maximum impact, responsibility for employee engagement should be organization wide. Indeed, in the best organizations, a culture of open communication begins with the CEO and other top executives, who know that employees must be engaged so they will contribute to the organization's goals. Internal communication processes are in place to ensure that employees understand the mission and how they fit into it.

> A culture of open communication begins with the CEO and other top executives.

Organizations with an open communication culture invest in a range of platforms to support dialogue and promote engagement. Meetings, web casts, executive presentations, newsletters, feedback mechanisms, forums, company blogs, and other interactive media are examples of formal internal channels designed to build engagement. As a vice president of an energy company said, "The more employees understand and feel like they're contributing or in line with the company strategy, the more productive they are and the higher the morale and [the] lower [the] turnover."[12]

In addition to developing and maintaining formal platforms such as these, an organization that recognizes the importance of communication will encourage its project managers to develop and maintain informal platforms. After all, an organization's culture is greatly affected by managers' daily interpersonal interactions. Honest, frequent communication keeps everyone informed about the organization's goals and how everyone can contribute to reaching the goals. Bronson Methodist Hospital in Kalamazoo, Michigan, is one organization that found no need for periodic formal meetings with the CEO after they built communication into the culture of their organization. As routine communication improved, attendance at the meetings with the CEO dwindled to nothing. "We already know what's going on" was the employees' explanation.[13]

In summary, consistent, honest, and frequent managerial communication has powerful benefits. When employees believe their manager supports them, they respond by becoming more committed and engaged in their job. In short, a project manager's daily informal communication behavior fosters engagement (1) within the team, (2) between the project manager and the team, and (3) between the team and the sponsoring organization.

Rapport

So far our examination of key contributors to project managers' competency in informal interpersonal communication has focused on trust, EI, and engagement. The following section of this chapter explores a fourth key contributor—rapport—and describes strategies and techniques for building rapport with team members and other stakeholders. The strategies are both verbal and nonverbal. The section begins with an overview of empathy, which is the foundation of rapport.

Empathy

Empathy is different from neutrality. Managers who strive to be neutral are instead expressing a lack of concern for the well-being of others,

Table 4.3 Examples of statements reflecting neutrality vs. empathy

Neutrality	Empathy
That really isn't much of a problem.	Sounds like you're really concerned about the situation. Tell me more.
Everyone has to face that at one time or another.	That can be a tough situation. Here's how I've seen it handled, but I want you to give me your reaction.
Well, everyone is entitled to an opinion.	I think we disagree. Let's discuss this further and compare viewpoints.

whereas managers who strive to be empathic are showing that they identify with the other person's problem, share their feelings, and accept the emotional values involved. Compare the examples in Table 4.3. Empathic statements are more likely to contribute to rapport, and rapport is a key contributor to an open communication climate.

Empathy throughout the Project's Life Cycle. As a manager, you will begin to foster the development of empathy among your project team members when you first form the team and assign the project. The proximity and forced interaction will pave the way toward empathic relationships. That's because they will find common ground. Further, as they engage with each other and with you, they will become more emotionally invested in the organization as well as the project. Ultimately, the organization will become smarter and more effective because the work of the organization is done through person-to-person relationships.

As the project progresses, there are more ways to encourage empathy. For instance, you can gather stakeholders to celebrate a milestone, achievement, holiday, or even a birthday. That will give everyone an opportunity to exchange perceptions and learn about each other in a low-stress environment. Informal, face-to-face interactions work best for developing empathy because both verbal and nonverbal cues are exchanged; the combination gives a more complete understanding of the information being shared.

"Lean" communication channels such as virtual meetings, text messages, and e-mail exchanges are a poor substitute for face-to-face interactions. If your people are scattered in the field or telecommuting from remote locations, it's much more difficult for them to develop empathic relationships. Be creative and try to get everyone together from time to time. The benefits will be worth the cost.

Empathy and the Amount of Information. Empathic project managers are sensitive to the amount of information their various audiences want and need. Too often a deluge of data will overwhelm and confuse. Project managers should put themselves in their audience's shoes and ask, "What information is relevant to their work? What do they care to know?" Do not overwhelm your workers with mountains of raw data but, rather, convey to them useful information in a timely manner—and make sure your communication is a two-way street.[14]

Nonverbal Communication

When building rapport, pay attention to your nonverbal behavior as well as your verbal behavior. The old saying that a picture speaks a thousand words is still true. How you look and how you sound contribute more to the impression you create than what you say. Therefore, when interacting with your team, sponsors, and other stakeholders are sending messages, it's important to show attention with your whole body, not just your words.

Similarly, whenever you send messages to others at work, the receivers will be reading your nonverbal behaviors. They will judge you on two dimensions: *competence* and *warmth*. Competence gets to how smart, able, and skilled your receivers think you are. Warmth is about how nice, engaging, and friendly they think you are. Obviously, for maximum success in communication, the goal is to demonstrate competence and warmth through your nonverbal behavior. The problem is that, typically, as confidence goes up, warmth goes down, especially for women in business and professional settings.

Here are some nonverbal behaviors that contribute to building rapport. These subtle behaviors will help you project both competence and warmth, whether you are speaking or listening. First, practice eye contact with everyone in the room. Avoid sweeping back and forth with your eyes like a windshield wiper, but instead hold eye contact with each person for a few seconds. Be mindful that eye contact patterns are different for speaking and for listening—in the United States, listeners look more than speakers do. Eye contact also differs from culture to culture—for instance, the Japanese are generally less comfortable with extended eye contact than are Americans. Other nonverbal signals are also important to the attitude we convey, though their interpretation and impact will vary across cultures.

Nonverbal Expressions of Competence and Warmth:

- Eye contact
- Hand gestures
- Head tilt
- Posture and distance

A second nonverbal technique to build the impression of competence and warmth is to keep your hands in front of your torso, elbows bent and palms open. This pose allows you to gesture easily when speaking to reinforce your words. Avoid pointing at people, which is considered aggressive and dominant in many cultures. Keeping your hands open rather than clutching an object, fiddling with objects, or tenting your fingers, looks more relaxed and receptive.

Third, be aware of how you hold your head. Tilting it makes you seem attentive, especially when combined with eye contact. Nodding your head as you listen can encourage the other person to continue speaking. However, constant nodding looks habitual and can be distracting, thereby working against your intended impression. Be aware that some cultures interpret a nod to mean, "I agree," not just "I'm listening." In addition, there are gender differences in the use of these nonverbal behaviors, with women typically tilting and nodding more than men do as they listen.

A fourth nonverbal technique is to maintain a posture that makes you look involved, alert, and open. Whether standing or sitting, keep your body relaxed, leaning slightly in as you listen and speak. The distance you are expected to maintain during conversation varies from culture to culture. In the U.S. business environment, "social distance" is typically 3 to 5 feet. Getting within arm's reach is considered "intimate"; it can also be interpreted as aggressive and asserting power or authority. On the other hand, staying five feet apart is considered "public," too formal for interaction in small groups. Be sensitive to cultural preferences when seeking a comfortable distance.

In short, project managers' nonverbal behaviors when speaking and listening will contribute significantly to an empathic impression. Empathy, as we have seen, builds rapport with managers' communication partners. And rapport, like engagement and trust, are the building blocks of an open communication environment. An open communication environment will ensure success throughout a project's life cycle.

Verbal Communication

As a project progresses through its stages, you and your team are bound to face a number of challenges. Uncertainties, ambiguities, unforeseen roadblocks, and changes all lead to stress, which threatens an open communication environment. If, for instance, you notice that people are not talking in meetings, don't assume that all is well. The channels are closing down. But if you have built strong rapport among the team members and stakeholders, you can minimize the negative consequences of stressful challenges to your project.

Maintain rapport by encouraging the receivers of your message to engage in conversation, especially when the topic is negative. Here are some techniques you can use to verify, reduce misunderstanding, and increase motivation.

Verbal Strategies for Building Rapport:

- Ask open questions
- Answer questions
- Check understanding
- Use familiar terms

Ask Open Questions. "Do you understand?" is not a great question. Naturally, people will say "yes," pretending that they do understand you rather than admitting that they don't, which would imply that (a) your communication skills are poor, or (b) their listening skills are poor. To maintain rapport, ask an open question that implies neither of these weaknesses. Open questions call for a long response rather than a one-word response such as "yes" or "no." Open questions will keep the conversation going. Open questions like, "What part of what I've said should I talk about some more?" or "What more can I add?" encourage listeners to talk without fear of criticism.

Answer Questions. During stressful stages of a project's life cycle, teams and stakeholders are likely to ask questions. Your responses should aim for clarity and completeness. Never respond to a request for information with a putdown like, "I've already answered that." If they are asking, they probably don't know the answer and will resent the implication that they should know it. Maintaining rapport means that you are patient and forthcoming with information. And when you don't have the information being requested, try to say when you will get it and share it with them.

Check Understanding. As a sender, it is helpful to ask the recipient of the message to paraphrase the message to indicate how it was understood, with specific focus on what needs to be done ("What is the most important take away for you?"). You can check by inviting questions ("Who would like to ask the first question?") and summaries ("Who will summarize what our next step will be?")

Use Familiar Terms. A final verbal strategy for maintaining rapport is simple but often overlooked. This strategy applies especially when communicating with external stakeholders. Periodically, project managers and their teams communicate with external stakeholders such as clients, contractors, vendors, regulatory agencies, and end users. External stakeholders are unlikely to be as familiar with jargon, acronyms, and technical language as internal audiences are. Therefore, project managers and teams can maintain rapport by being careful to define terms and use examples that their external listeners can identify with. Being subjected to unfamiliar in-group language is annoying and threatening to rapport.

To summarize, supportive communication is critical to maintaining rapport and productivity while addressing the project's problem. A director and board member of the Project Management Institute Global Accreditation Center and professor at Western Carolina University, Vittal Anantatmula[15] identified eight strategies for supportive communication behavior (see Table 4.4).

Table 4.4 Attributes of supportive communication

Assess objectively	As the project manager, you communicate the incident objectively and offer a solution.
Be honest	Your message, thoughts, and feelings must align completely.
Integrate	Assimilate a current situation or issue at hand with the past and related communication.
Focus on the positive	Place emphasis on areas of agreements and strengths and communicate with respect to work collaboratively.
Focus on the problem	Separate the person from the issue at hand.
Take responsibility	Take responsibility for your actions and words by using "I" language wherever applicable.
Focus on specifics	Focus on specific issues and avoid the temptation to generalize or make extreme statements.
Listen supportively	Listen without interrupting, process the message for objective understanding, address relevant issues or concerns for an accurate understanding of the message.

Summary

This chapter describes informal interpersonal communication situations that project managers routinely engage in and provides practical strategies, techniques, and methods that will ensure the success of the interactions. Four key informal interpersonal communication competencies are examined: developing trust, developing EI, increasing employee engagement, and building rapport. First, trust is crucial in both directions—the manager must trust the team, and the team must trust the manager. Second, EI is defined. By improving their ability to recognize and understand emotions, project managers can do a much better job of managing social interactions. Third, nonverbal and verbal behaviors that increase employee engagement are described. Engaged workers are committed, involved, enthusiastic, and productive. Fourth, strategies are presented that build and maintain rapport within the team, between the team and the project manager, and between the project team and external stakeholders.

Questions

1. The section on developing trust in this chapter presents several strategies. Which one seems to be the most relevant to your attempts to build trust with a colleague or team mate? How will you apply it?

2. The section on emotional intelligence (EI) in this chapter explains the importance of listening to informal communication—the grapevine. Describe an example of grapevine information that affected your work on a project team.

3. As you read the section on employee engagement in this chapter, which principle applies best to your own work experience? Analyze the communication behavior of one of your managers that resulted in your decreased engagement. What would have helped to improve the situation?

4. The section on rapport in this chapter claims that empathy is the foundation of rapport. If you work with someone so different from you that you are struggling to find empathy, what are some techniques that you can try to overcome this challenge, become empathic, and establish rapport?

CHAPTER 5

Project Success in a Global Context

Chapter Objectives

The purpose of this chapter is to help project managers learn strategies and techniques for communicating with stakeholders in a global context. Specifically, project managers will learn how to:

- Communicate with distributed teams
- Use traditional and emerging communication technology
- Develop culturally sensitive project teams
- Apply PMI standards for ethical and professional conduct when communicating

Vittal S. Anantatmula, a leading expert on project management, notes that "A free-market philosophy, a technology-aided global economy, and increased international business and competition are encouraging organizations to ignore national boundaries and collaborate globally, often virtually."[1] The benefits of global collaboration projects include lowering costs, increasing revenue, and sharing technical expertise for mutual gains and technology transfer.

This chapter considers four major trends in the global work environment: growing reliance on teams and cross-boundary collaboration, increasing reliance on technology, expanding project teams' cultural sensitivity, and heightened emphasis on ethics. Table 5.1 summarizes the trends and introduces implications for your success as a project manager.

Table 5.1 Trends in global business and implications for project managers

Trend	Implications for managers
Increasing collaboration of distributed teams	• Use social media/collaboration tools • Provide training
Increasing reliance on technology	• Become media sensitive • Use appropriate technology
Increasing sensitivity to cultural differences	• Learn another language • Create a welcoming culture
Increasing emphasis on ethics	• Have a formal code of conduct • Broadcast it to everyone

Communicating with Distributed Teams

It's easy to see why teams have been adopted as a key work structure in contemporary organizations. Today's workplace is fast paced and intense. Many organizations have replaced a bureaucratic hierarchy with flexible, cooperative, mission-driven teams led by managers who expect their team members to participate fully in the project.

As a project manager, you encourage collaboration and group loyalty among your team members every day. The focus is on using two-way communication tools to encourage input and keep everyone informed, thereby creating a sense of community and a collaborative culture.

> Distributed teams use social media tools to support collaboration.

When your team members are on the road, geographically scattered, or on flexible schedules, communication challenges are even greater. If face-to-face interactions are not practical, you can use social enterprise tools like Facebook at Work, Yammer, or Jive to connect people. Streaming video and instant messaging (IM) are well suited to building community.

A 2013 survey of 651 organizations in a range of industries and global regions found that the majority of employers (56 percent) use social media to communicate with employees on topics such as organizational culture, team building, change management, and innovation. Furthermore, 70 percent of the survey respondents agreed that the use of internal social business/collaboration tools had a positive impact on employee productivity.[2] The more managers use these tools, the more adept they become at fostering collaboration. When employees connect, either in person or through technologies, they can establish dialogues and collaboration rather than relying on top-down, one-way communication. The manager of the future must know how to support collaboration in distributed teams.

Leading Distributed Teams

Managing distributed teams calls for special communication skills. First, it's important to select team members who communicate information freely and honestly. Once your team is in place, here are some other strategies that will support collaboration:

- **Be a facilitator.** Managing teams is less about supervising than it is about motivating members to do their best. Avoid the tendency to micromanage once you have defined the team's objectives and responsibilities.
- **Support the team.** Provide resources, run interference, and resolve internal conflicts. Give them all the information they need, and more, to encourage trust. Remember that people cannot work in a vacuum.
- **Delegate.** Managers occasionally have trouble admitting that they cannot do it all. Instead of trying to manage every aspect of a project, trust team members to perform their assigned tasks, especially in agile environments, as discussed in Chapter 2. Trust also builds respect for you as the project manager and maintains morale.
- **Seek diversity.** Heterogeneous teams experience more conflict but often produce higher-quality results than homogeneous teams. Stress the importance of collaboration, flexibility, and openness toward unfamiliar viewpoints and work styles.[3]

Tips for Managing Work Teams:

- Be a facilitator
- Support the team
- Delegate
- Seek diversity

Communicating with Culturally Diverse Distributed Teams

In teams or work groups that are culturally diverse, you may have to deal with communication difficulties and language barriers, which decrease cohesion. Be sure your team members put teammates at ease by respecting the conventions of each culture. Writing styles, for example, differ across cultures. A direct, concise e-mail may be standard in the United States, but Japanese recipients may consider it rude and vulgar. That's why a project manager recently sent an e-mail to a Japanese colleague that began with, "The local cherry blossoms are particularly beautiful this spring."

Fluency may be a roadblock for transnational team members communicating in English. As the project manager, you can build in more time during teleconferences and perhaps hire translators. Nonverbal behavior also varies from culture to culture, as described in Chapter 2. For example, in the United States, business professionals usually shake hands when they "seal a deal," but unrelated men and women are forbidden to touch in Islamic countries.

Videoconferencing tools allow your team to see and hear each other's nonverbal cues including posture, facial expression, and voice tone, yet the risk of misunderstanding remains strong. As a manager, you must decide whether these more expensive methods of communication are worth the attempt to reduce the assumptions and barriers involved. Cultural diversity training can reduce the likelihood of misunderstandings and blunders among your team.

Best Practices for Communicating with Distributed Teams

Given that your primary communication goal for managing distributed, culturally diverse teams is to foster collaboration, several communication tools are readily available. The following paragraphs suggest do's and don'ts for the use of texting, social media, and blogs.[4]

Best Practices for Electronic Messaging. Texting and IM are common ways for distributed teams to exchange short messages. Advantages include ease of implementation, speed, ability to archive messages, and efficiency. These tools allow the team to immediately ask and answer questions, exchange comments informally, and have a record of the conversation. Disadvantages include lack of security, lack of structure and formality, and distractions.

The instant, personal messages typically exchanged via text and IM often are casual in tone and may contain typos as well as grammar and punctuation errors, indicating that senders did not take/have time to edit for corrections before sending the message. Although slang and acronyms may increase the speed of interactions, they do not project professionalism and they may result in misunderstanding. Table 5.2 summarizes some best practices for texting and IM'ing to build collaboration of distributed teams.

Table 5.2 Best practices for texting and IM

Archive all incoming and outgoing messages
Develop an electronic messaging policy and circulate it among the team
Do not use text or instant messaging for highly sensitive communication
Limit proprietary information
Be concise, but be sure acronyms, abbreviations, jargon are familiar to all
Use punctuation for clarity and accuracy
Avoid emoticons and formatting for emphasis (all caps, multiple exclamation points)

Best Practices for Social Networks. Corporate intranets have evolved into enterprise social networks like Slack, Office 365, and Facebook for Business. Other firms are using internal social networks for communication, collaboration, and project management. Enterprise social networks allow teams to share calendars, work on shared files, ask questions, and crowd source ideas.

External social networks allow organizations to interact with their audiences quickly, informally, and in an environment that stakeholders are comfortable. Facebook, Instagram, Pinterest, LinkedIn, and Twitter

Table 5.3 Best practices for social networking

Internal social networks	External social networks
Use instead of meetings for simple and quick progress updates, information sharing, and gathering of feedback	Tell compelling stories in a conversational tone. Use a consistent brand voice across networks
Give the online community time to grow	Focus on customers' needs and provide content they care about
Find internal influencers to lead discussions and generate interest	Respond quickly to comments and questions, whether positive or critical
Set guidelines for information than can and cannot be shared with others in the organization	Develop a social media disaster plan

allow communication with external stakeholders as well as marketing to customers.

Disadvantages of social networking include one-way messaging and loss of control. Best practices for use of internal and external social networks are summarized in Table 5.3.

Best Practices for Blogs. Blogs are websites that are updated frequently. A descendant of diaries and online journals, organizational blogs feature short, concise posts and images that appear chronologically. Blogs are commonly used by project teams as a coordination tool, to share information, or to provide progress updates. The team members, managers, and other stakeholders who have been given access to the blog can view all the information. The benefit of blogs as a project coordination tool is amplified for distributed teams.

Blogs can also be used internally as a means of sharing information and collecting feedback from stakeholders. Blogs allow everyone to participate in the discussion at will and keep a permanent record of all the thoughts, comments, and input that can be reviewed and considered at the decision maker's convenience.

External blogs are often used to promote the organization and develop relationships with a variety of audiences. Blog communication is viewed as more authentic than the rote and often dry language of mission statements and formal press releases. Blogs are written in a conversational tone, which external stakeholders often view favorably. Composing posts that connect with readers' interests and responding directly to comments

Table 5.4 Best practices for blogging

Internal blogs	External blogs
Use for simple and quick progress updates, information sharing, and gathering of feedback	Use for quick release of information during crises
To encourage honesty, do not censor bloggers	Be sure that postings are consistent with the company's brand, mission, and image
Write in a conversational tone	Monitor blogs daily to keep abreast of public sentiment
Maintain a professional writing style, remembering that posts are permanent records	Respond quickly to publicly posted blog comments, whether positive or critical

can encourage customers to remain engaged with the organization, its products, or projects in development. Blogs also offer organizations a chance to learn about criticisms and crises quickly and respond almost immediately.

Disadvantages of blogging include permanence and loss of control. Best practices for use of internal and external blogs are summarized in Table 5.4.

Using Communication Technology

Let's review for a moment. This chapter is designed to help you manage project teams in a global context. The previous section focused on communicating with distributed teams, that is, teams that are geographically dispersed. Teams operating from different locations are becoming the norm in today's business world.

Recall that the Sequence for Success model that is at the heart of this book (Figure 5.1) illustrates the importance of interpersonal communication for project success. Face to face, formal and informal interactions lead to strong work relationships, which build loyalty, satisfaction, and commitment. Further, the model indicates that these positive emotions are prerequisites for maximum performance of the team and for organizational success. *The PMBOK® Guide—Sixth Edition* emphasizes that project managers should use interpersonal, face to face, communication for maximum effectiveness with their teams.[5] However, this channel is

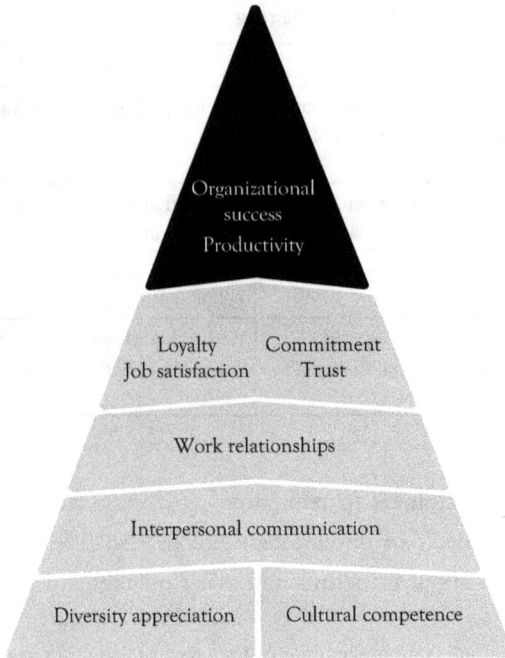

Figure 5.1 Productivity and the sequence for success

often impractical and unavailable to project managers of distributed teams. Instead, they must use communication technology. How can you maximize technological channels so they approximate the effectiveness of personal interaction? This section offers some suggestions and best practices for technological communication.

Advantages of Technological Communication

If you spend as much time as most managers do reading and responding to e-mail, texting your staff, blogging both internally and with external stakeholders, participating in webinars and virtual meetings, and compulsively checking your smartphone while sitting in traffic, you know that developments in technology will largely determine the future of business. In the words of Tom Friedman, columnist for the *New York Times* and winner of three Pulitzer Prizes, we have gone from a connected world to a hyper connected world in the last 10 years. Technology is an integral part of everyone's work life. The justifications for our increasing reliance on technology are (1) increased efficiency, (2) increased productivity, and (3) improved communication.

Advantages of Technology:

- Increased efficiency
- Increased productivity
- Improved communication

Disadvantages of Technological Communication

Technology is more than a beneficial tool; it's a force that must be constantly reassessed. Just because it's new, technology is not necessarily good. It's a thin line to walk, and it requires some creative thinking to stay balanced between technological advantage and overkill.

Communication technology can create certain disadvantages in organizations. Over-reliance on technology brings a danger of sensory overload, a decline in work relationships, and reduced opportunities for corrective feedback. The application of emerging technologies such as virtual reality will allow teams to meet in a virtual meeting room and "see" each other face-to-face. Should that become a reality, it will end the practice of dialing in from home while still in your PJs. On a more serious level, technological communication can result in worker isolation and disengagement. Team members' engagement is a critical factor for project success, as explained in Chapter 4.

Speaking of sensory overload, if you feel buried by e-mail these days, just wait. The majority of e-mail traffic is predicted to come from business e-mail rather than personal e-mail in the next few years. Business e-mail will account for a whopping 132 billion e-mails sent and received per day. Personal e-mail traffic, by contrast, is expected to decrease, with individuals opting to use social media, IM, and texting to communicate with friends and families.[6]

> Disadvantages of Technology:
>
> - Sensory overload
> - Weak work relationships
> - Reduced feedback

Despite the potential disadvantages of technology, networked organizations are the norm. The strategic decision for project managers is not *whether* to use technological channels but *which* channel is best for the situation and how to maximize its capabilities. The following paragraphs present guidelines for channel choice.

Guidelines for Channel Choice

As a project manager, you can't simply rely on the channel you feel most comfortable with when communicating; you need to consider the impression the channel makes with your intended audience. Here is a true story that demonstrates this idea. Once there was an accounting department manager who relied exclusively on sticky notes for communicating with her subordinates, to the extent that she would silently enter a worker's cubicle, stick a note onto the computer monitor, and silently leave again, while the subordinate sat right there. How do you think her employees felt about the manager and her message?

Different situations and messages call for different channels, as summarized in Table 5.5.

Table 5.5 Channel options for messages

Message type	Message example	Key channel characteristics	Channel example
Sensitive	Condolence	Broad bandwidth Feedback mechanism Symbolic importance	Face-to-face
Negative	Layoff	Broad bandwidth Feedback mechanism	Face-to-face Videoconference
Complex	Procedure	Permanence Feedback mechanism	Multiple channels

Routine	Meeting reminder	Low cost Efficiency	E-mail Text message
Persuasive	Sales	Broad bandwidth Interactive Symbolic importance Feedback mechanism	Face-to-face Videoconference
Need for immediate response	Question	Feedback mechanism Speed	Text message Instant message Face-to-face
Informative	New product	Permanence Accessibility	Blog E-mail Newsletter

When deciding which communication technology to use in a particular situation, the *PMBOK® Guide* suggests that managers consider the following factors:

1. ***Urgency of the need for information.*** Information frequency and format may vary at different stages of the project.
2. ***Availability and reliability of technology.*** The technology should be compatible and accessible for all stakeholders of the project.
3. ***Ease of use.*** The technology should be suitable for all participants and training should be offered where appropriate.
4. ***Project environment.*** The physical location of team members, their language proficiency, and their cultures may constrain the efficiency of communication technology.
5. ***Sensitivity and confidentiality of the information.*** Security may be required to protect proprietary information.

Factors Affecting Technology Choice:

- Urgency
- Availability and reliability
- Ease of use
- Environment
- Sensitivity and confidentiality

The range of communication technology choices can be daunting. Some commonly used technologies are listed in Table 5.5. Others are cutting edge and just emerging. Let us consider two scenarios that illustrate how a project manager selects the best channel for communicating with the team.

Block chain. The first scenario involves block chain, an emerging technology. Let's say you are the manager of a complex industrial project. Your planning has included developing a work breakdown structure that lists all of the tasks required to complete the project. You have assigned responsibility and timeframes for those tasks. You began at the big picture level and then divided each task into individual sub-projects with specific responsibilities assigned. You developed a critical path and even constructed a Gantt or PERT chart to list all of the tasks, timeframes, and responsibilities.

Frequently much of your communication about progress in completing tasks and sub-projects occurs in periodic meetings. But this periodic updating has sometimes created problems for downstream tasks and sub-projects that cannot begin until certain upstream tasks and sub-projects are completed. You realize that you need a means for providing near-real-time information to improve communication, increase efficiency, and help keep the project on schedule. Perhaps block chain is a solution to your problem.

"A block chain is a database that is shared across a network of computers. Once a record has been added to the chain it is very difficult to change. To ensure all the copies of the database are the same, the network makes constant checks."[7] Using block chain, sub-project and task managers you can enter current status information and near-real-time updates on progress into blocks that the entire project team can see but not alter. This can be helpful for managers of sub-projects that cannot begin until a previous sub-project or task has been completed. Block chain use also can help you and your team stage materials, free up time for necessary personnel, and other pre-start planning activities. Another benefit is that it can alert everyone to unexpected delays which can provide more time for coordination with other task managers to ensure the project due date is met.

Teleconferencing. Here is another example of decision making about technologically mediated communication, this one focusing on more traditional channels. Let's say you are a project manager working in a nonprofit organization who needs to hold a routine meeting with your geographically dispersed team. The team members are located in different cities, and you have decided that the most relevant of the five factors listed in the *PMBOK® Guide—Sixth Edition* are urgency and reliability. As a result, you have narrowed your choices to video networking, videoconferencing, and audio conferencing. At first you are tempted to use videoconferencing because it provides visual cues in addition to audio cues. Then you consider video networking, which not only provides real-time interactive video and audio, it also offers data sharing via the Internet.

However, in this situation the effort to set up online collaboration tools and videoconferences may not be justified. Sharing data and files in real time during a routine meeting may not be important. Even visual information may be of little value; it might distract from the critical message. Considering cost, time, and the amount of information that needs to be shared, you decide to use the simplest technology, an audio conference, as the most effective.

Importance of Media Sensitivity for Project Managers

The previous two channel choice scenarios are designed to illustrate a fairly complex decision process. How important is it for project managers to go through these steps when selecting a communication medium? Several studies have identified a strong correlation between a manager's media sensitivity and managerial performance. For instance, in one study, when a task involved complex information or was highly emotional, effective managers were more inclined than were ineffective managers to use communication channels with a broad bandwidth, or capacity to carry information, such as face-to-face conversation.[8] So if you want to be successful at work, you should try to gain media sensitivity.

Successful managers are media-sensitive managers.

Ethical Issues for Technological Communication

Media sensitivity includes guiding your team in the proper, ethical use of communication technology. For instance, IM is an official corporate communication tool for over one-fourth of U.S. companies, yet many don't have an official IM policy, risking breaches of confidentiality, viruses, and copyright infringement. New communication tools are constantly becoming available, requiring strategic decisions about their use. Your team relies on you for training and for modeling ethical use of technology.

Surveillance of Technology Use. A second ethical issue relevant to communication technology is that monitoring mechanisms are developing right along with innovations in technology and becoming more sophisticated every year. For example, federal law enforcement and national security offices have sweeping authority to monitor Internet communications, including encrypted e-mails, social networking websites, and peer-to-peer software such as Skype and Zoom. In the United States, phone and broadband networks have been required to have government interception capabilities since 1994, under a law called the Communications Assistance to Law Enforcement Act.

The business sector is following the example of government surveillance policies by developing technologies that allow them to eavesdrop on employees. Electronic surveillance systems allow employers to gather very detailed information about how their employees spend their time at work.[9] Companies monitor employees for many reasons. These include:

- Preventing lawsuits
- Reducing the misuse of company resources
- Protecting intellectual property[10]

Companies have invested in technology that can do much more than block access to certain Internet sites. They frequently have the ability to record every key stroke ever typed on a worker's computer (even ones that have been deleted).

Assume your technology use at work is being monitored.

A survey of more than 700 companies by the Society for Human Resource Management (SHRM) found that:

- Almost 75 percent of the companies monitor their workers' Internet use.
- 43 percent monitor their workers' e-mail.
- 45 percent monitor phone use.
- 45 percent track content, keystrokes, and time spent at the keyboard.[11]

Monitoring by employers is supported by the courts. Furthermore, employers need not alert employees to the fact that they are watching. Only two states, Delaware and Connecticut, require employers to notify employees of monitoring. According to a recent American Management Association survey:

- 17 percent of employers do not inform workers that the company is monitoring content, keystrokes and time spent at the keyboard.
- 16 percent do not let employees know the company reviews computer activity.
- 29 percent do not alert employees to e-mail monitoring.[12]

Your team should realize that any time spent using technology at work must be limited to work-related activities. Further, any messages they send or receive at work should be appropriate for anyone to read. In 2010, in its first ruling on the privacy rights of employees who send messages on the job, the Supreme Court unanimously agreed that supervisors may read through subordinates' text messages if they suspect that work rules are being violated. So remind your team to be on their best behavior and to think twice before communicating something even a little bit questionable while on the job.

Developing Culturally Sensitive Project Teams

This section of the chapter narrows the focus to what is arguably the toughest but most important strategy for success, developing your cultural sensitivity, and offers tools to help you reach that goal. Further, it presents ideas for developing cultural sensitivity among your project team members, so they, too, can be successful in a global work environment.

Types of Diversity

The data confirm what we have all already noticed in our own organizations—diversity is a reality along the dimensions of gender, age, education, and culture. Why is diversity a competitive advantage? Because organizations with diversity tend to be more creative and more profitable. Varied perspectives help them design products and services that have global appeal.

Since the payoff of a diverse workforce depends not on the diversity itself but on promoting a sense of belonging, you must use tact when managing a team whose members may be different from you and one another.

Culturally Sensitive Communication. Despite the fact that diverse workforces are the norm, a 2013 Towers Watson Global Workforce Study shows that only about half of today's managers are viewed as effective by their subordinates when it comes to their skill at listening to different points of view and working across cultural differences.[13] Clearly the gap must be closed. The strategies described in this section will help you develop a welcoming culture that values individuals regardless of skin, intellect, talents, gender, or years. As a manager, you must be able to connect with others in a deep and direct way and develop relationships that will bridge differences.

DIVERSITY = Different Individuals Valuing Each other Regardless of Skin, Intellect, Talents, or Years

---

Bridging differences takes social and emotional intelligence, as described in Chapter 4. Cross-cultural competence involves awareness of differences and the ability to capitalize on those differences. Misunderstandings and communication breakdowns may also be due to differences in the degree of directness, appropriate subjects for conversation, touch, loudness and pitch, even silence.

Linguistic skills strongly affect cultural awareness. In her autobiography, U.S. Supreme Court Justice Sonia Sotomayor describes her struggles as a child in the South Bronx—she spoke only Spanish at home but attended classes taught only in English. Sotomayor argues that language is "a code of the soul" that unlocks the music, poetry, history, and literature of a culture, "but it is also a prison."

Justice Sotomayor learned early "that things break down [when] people can't imagine someone else's point of view."[14] Learning at least a little about another language is a practical way to improve interpersonal communication in diverse teams. Learning another language also indicates that you are aware of and accept another culture's values, traditions, and world view.

Speech and language differences, nonverbal behavior such as eye contact, and facial expressions all complicate the communication process in cross-cultural situations. In summary, to improve your communication with culturally diverse workers:

- Check for possible language differences as the source of misunderstanding.
- Look for possible cultural sources of misunderstanding.
- Acknowledge your communication mistakes and correct them.
- Correct others' inappropriate communication behavior.

Self-Assessment Tools

Before you can reach your goal, you have to identify where you are now. Self-assessment can be an uncomfortable process, but it's the way forward.

The Diversity Awareness Continuum. Here is a quick and easy tool for determining your starting point in developing cultural sensitivity (Table 5.6). Read and react to each sentence in the left-hand column by putting an X in one of the middle column spaces that best reflects where you fit. Then draw your profile by connecting your Xs.

Now that you know the starting point, it's easy to find your end point or goal. The closer your line is to the right-hand column, the greater your awareness and sensitivity regarding diversity. The closer to the left-hand column, the less aware you may be about diversity-related issues. Your goal is to move closer to the right-hand column on each dimension.

Table 5.6 Diversity awareness continuum

	1	2	3	4	5	
I don't know about the cultural norms of different groups in my organization	—	—	—	—	—	I know about the cultural norms of different groups in my organization
I don't hold stereotypes about other groups	—	—	—	—	—	I admit my stereotypes about other groups
I feel partial to, and more comfortable with, some groups than others	—	—	—	—	—	I feel equally comfortable with all groups
I gravitate toward others who are like me	—	—	—	—	—	I gravitate toward others who are different from me
I prefer managing a homogeneous team	—	—	—	—	—	I prefer managing a multicultural team
I feel that everyone is the same, with similar values and preferences	—	—	—	—	—	I feel that everyone is unique, with different values and preferences
I'm confused by the culturally different behaviors I see among staff	—	—	—	—	—	I understand the cultural influences behind some of the behaviors I see among staff
I get irritated when confronted by someone who does not speak English	—	—	—	—	—	I show patience and understanding with limited English speakers
I'm task focused and don't like to waste time chatting	—	—	—	—	—	I find that more gets done when I spend time on relationships first
I feel that newcomers to this society should comply with our rules	—	—	—	—	—	I feel that both newcomers and their employer organizations need to change to fit together

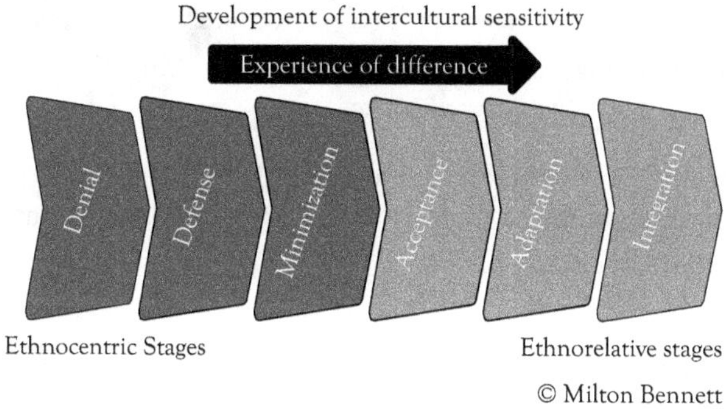

Development of intercultural sensitivity

Ethnocentric Stages   Ethnorelative stages

© Milton Bennett

Figure 5.2 Bennett's model

Bennett's Model. Milton Bennett designed a six-stage developmental model of cultural sensitivity, reflected in Figure 5.2.

Bennett's model provides another tool you might find useful for self-assessment. You will note that the first three stages in the model are "ethnocentric": *denial, defense,* and *minimization.* An example of a *denial* statement is, "No matter where you go, a smile will open all doors." At the second stage, *defense,* you are aware of differences but hostile toward other cultures, so you might say, "Our way is the right way." At the third stage, *minimization,* the differences you are aware of are superficial, so you might say something like, "When dining with my Chinese team member, I'll use chopsticks."

Ethnocentric managers may acknowledge the existence of cultural differences but see their culture as the best in the world and look down on others as inferior because they are different. For whatever reasons, the ethnocentric manager builds resentment rather than good relationships.

Stages of Ethnocentrism:

1. Denial
2. Defense
3. Minimization

On the other hand, Bennett identified three ethnorelative stages: *acceptance, adaptation,* and *integration* (Figure 5.2). An example of a statement by a manager at the *acceptance* stage is, "I see why we have belief differences," or "Differences are OK." If you are at Bennett's *adaptation* stage, you can empathize, so you might say something like, "I will adopt some aspects of a culture," or "Differences enhance the workplace." If you are at Bennett's *integration* stage, you have developed the ability to embrace and capitalize on differences. An example statement at this stage is, "We're not a melting pot. Let's go for the stir-fry."

Stages of Ethnorelativism:

4. Acceptance
5. Adaptation
6. Integration

An ethnorelativistic manager recognizes and respects cultural differences and finds ways to make the workplace amenable to all.[15] Try plotting your course for cultural sensitivity by identifying where you are on the following flowchart (Figure 5.3), which is based on Bennett's model.

Your Improvement Plan

If you nodded your head as you read the previous paragraphs and thought, "Yes, these are all worthy goals," you now are probably thinking. "Now, how can I get there?" Simply, you will get there by taking one step at a time. Your personal improvement plan will work if it's action-oriented and ongoing.

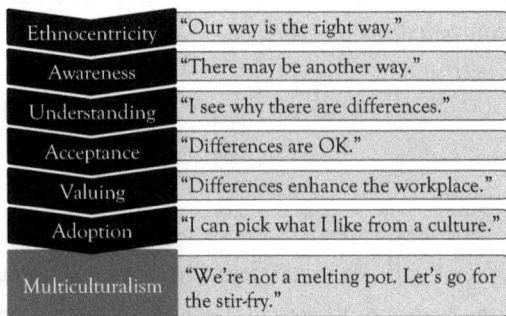

Ethnocentricity	"Our way is the right way."
Awareness	"There may be another way."
Understanding	"I see why there are differences."
Acceptance	"Differences are OK."
Valuing	"Differences enhance the workplace."
Adoption	"I can pick what I like from a culture."
Multiculturalism	"We're not a melting pot. Let's go for the stir-fry."

Figure 5.3 Developing cultural sensitivity

Here's how: At the beginning of next month, sit down and write out three things you plan to do that month—one new action for professional improvement, one for personal improvement, and one for relationship improvement. Next to each new behavior write down in what situation and with whom you will do it. Table 5.7 shows you how to organize your personal improvement plan. It shouldn't take you more than about 10 minutes.

Table 5.7 My action plan for the month

	Goal	Who	When	Where	What I'll say/do
Professional					
Personal					
Relationship					

On the last day of next month, check your list to see how well you met those three goals. If you didn't succeed, try to figure out why not. Then, construct a new action plan consisting of three things you plan to do the following month, taking into account the roadblocks from last month. This system should keep you on track for developing cultural competencies that are important for your career.

Developing Culturally Sensitive Teams

Once you've worked on your own cultural competence, it's time to address your team's awareness. You don't have to send them abroad to develop their cultural sensitivity. There are several things you can do to help your project team accept diversity.

Sending them to a cross-cultural communication training program is a good plan if one is available. However, a recent study published by The Economist Intelligence Unit found that almost half (47 percent) of companies don't invest in such training, though they recognize the benefits of overcoming cultural and communication barriers.[16]

Here are some other actions you might take that will help the project team develop cultural sensitivity:

- *Acknowledge the presence of culture differences*. Talk about differences in beliefs, values, goals, behaviors, and

language. Try to understand and explain the reasons for
these differences.

- ***Insist on a respectful environment.*** Be a role model by
  always using diversity-sensitive language yourself. Monitor
  others' language, humor, and stories and point out the impact
  of insensitive and offensive talk.
- ***Promote the benefits of diversity.*** Create and maintain
  heterogeneous teams. Be sure to consider age and gender
  as well as ethnicity and national origin when forming heterogeneous workgroups. Encourage multiple viewpoints
  during team meetings. Discourage groupthink and premature
  decision-making.

Ways to Encourage Your Project Team's Cultural Competence:

- Acknowledge differences
- Insist on respect for differences
- Promote the benefits of diversity

The Bottom Line: Culturally Sensitive Teams

Developing cultural sensitivity in yourself and your project team is an
ongoing process. The platform that fosters this process is daily interpersonal communication. A look to the future reveals a continued strong
relationship between effective interpersonal communication and organizational success. In fact, organizations with highly effective communicators are three and a half times more likely to significantly outperform their
industry peers than organizations whose leaders are poor communicators.

What does "effective communication" mean in a culturally diverse
context? It begins with a deep understanding of the organization's culture
and the workers' cultures, because that knowledge allows leaders to create
messages that will drive worker behaviors toward the organization's goals.
A 2013 Towers Watson survey of 651 organizations worldwide found that
in highly effective organizations,

- 96 percent of managers act in support of the organization's
  vision and values

- 93 percent of managers deliver messages in a way that is meaningful for their work group
- 91 percent of managers work across cultural differences when determining procedures
- 90 percent of managers listen carefully to different points of view[17]

Data published by a Project Management Institute study indicate even more behaviors that distinguish effective business communicators:

- They communicate frequently with their staff about goals, budgets, schedules, and business benefits
- They communicate with sufficient clarity and detail
- They use non-technical language
- They tailor messages to different stakeholder groups
- They use appropriate settings or media[18]

Remember the Sequence for Success model introduced in Chapter 1 and referred to throughout this book? The model illustrates how your daily communication leads to strong relationships, which lead to loyalty, satisfaction, and commitment. These emotional conditions lead to productivity and organizational success (Figure 5.4).

The model illustrates that project managers will thrive during times of change if they are skillful communicators, emotionally intelligent, collaborative, and culturally sensitive. Following the Sequence for Success will enable you to use your effective communication skills to produce the bottom-line results that will make your project a success.

The Project Manager's Responsibilities

To summarize, in order to thrive in the diverse business environment of tomorrow, project managers must be culturally sensitive. Improving your cultural sensitivity begins with self-awareness. This section presented two tools that will facilitate self-assessment of cultural sensitivity and help you set realistic, concrete goals. Next, the section considered ways to translate cultural attitudes and values into managerial behaviors. Instead of a universalist approach, which calls for treating everyone the same, or a

Figure 5.4 Sequence for success

particularist approach, which calls for individually different treatment, project managers need to be flexible and to accommodate the cultural values and practices of the team.

Third, this section examined strategies for developing cultural sensitivity in the project team, which include formal training, zero-tolerance for disrespect, openly discussing differences, and promoting the benefits of diversity. Following these strategies will enable you to use your effective communication skills to produce the bottom-line results that will make both you and your organization successful.

PMI Standards for Ethical and Professional Conduct

The final section of this chapter examines the importance of project managers' ethical conduct when communicating with their team and other stakeholders.

Heightened Emphasis on Ethics

If you paid any attention at all to the major corporate scandals in the early 21st century, you know how dangerous unethical behavior can be. Executives at Adelphia, Arthur Andersen, Enron, WorldCom, Martha Stewart Omnimedia, HealthSouth, and other corporations were charged with major ethics violations—accounting fraud, stock manipulation, obstructing justice, lying, and so on. Many of the accused executives were convicted, and some of their companies were even destroyed. In 2016, Wells Fargo admitted that some employees had created fake accounts to meet quotas; in 2017 the company admitted that employees also had sold customers car insurance that they didn't need. Such events have triggered increased emphasis on ethical standards.

The Sarbanes-Oxley Act of 2002 requires companies to develop a code of ethics applicable to employees and directors. Today, 93 percent of the Fortune 100 companies publish a code of ethics or conduct or a values statement. Furthermore, 58 percent of the Fortune 100 companies that have a code of conduct extend it to vendors and contractor companies.

Sarbanes-Oxley also makes corporate leaders responsible for the unethical behavior of their employees—unless they can show that they provided adequate ethical training for them. As a result, 79 percent of the Fortune 100 companies require employee training on their code of ethics, with proof of completion.[19]

As a project manager, you face ethical dilemmas and temptations every day. Ethical issues range from corporate accounting practices to social media use by team members, to harassment, to pay equity. The importance of trust and a positive communication climate is discussed in Chapter 4. Unfortunately, it's difficult to develop trust when so many blatant examples of mistrust occur and when you face conflicting ethical demands. The only way to build trust is to follow the practices of ethical communication.

> The only way to build trust is to follow the practices of ethical communication.

Codes of Ethical and Professional Conduct

If your company has not developed a formal code of ethics, check to see whether your professional association has. For instance, the American Society for Quality specifies standards of behavior for quality management professionals. The Institute for Supply Management also developed a code of ethics relevant to supply chain managers' challenges.

The Project Management Institute publishes the *Code of Ethics and Professional Conduct* to instill confidence in the profession and to help project managers make good decisions, particularly when facing situations where they may be asked to compromise their values. The values that the global project management community defines as most important are responsibility, respect, fairness, and honesty. The *Code of Ethics and Professional Conduct* affirms these four values as its foundation and states that it is mandatory for members of PMI to act in compliance with these standards.

Project Management Values:

- Responsibility
- Respect
- Fairness
- Honesty

Alternatively, you can compose a code of conduct for yourself and your project team, perhaps with input from your human resources and legal departments. The code should clarify expectations of conduct and state that you expect your team to recognize the ethical dimensions of professional behavior and communication. Your code of conduct may be broad or specific regarding values, but at a minimum, it should address managerial communication and sensitivity to cultural differences. It should also spell out consequences of noncompliance with the standards. Finally, you should broadcast your code to all stakeholders and check that they understand it.

Project Managers' Ethical Behaviors

How do these codes of conduct translate into daily managerial behaviors? Kathryn Wells and Timothy Kloppenborg, experts in project management, identified a number of crucial activities that align with PMI's standards for ethical conduct. Among their guidelines for project managers are the following:

- Stand up for your team and their ideas.
- Serve your team rather than the other way around.
- Only promise what you can deliver and keep your promises.
- Do good quality work.
- Volunteer to help those who are struggling.
- Create psychological safety for your team members.

Further, Wells and Kloppenborg proposed several guidelines for a project manager's communication behavior that are consistent with PMI's standards:

- Communicate openly and honestly.
- Find the truth, then communicate it.
- Admit your mistakes.
- Treat everyone fairly.
- Speak calmly.
- Make requests instead of demands.
- Don't complain about what cannot be changed.
- Acknowledge when something is done well.
- Handle negative situations in a positive manner.[20]

Looking over this list of best practices, you may be thinking that they are easier said than done, especially the one about admitting mistakes. Newer managers, in particular, may fear that such communication behaviors could erode their image as a leader. But research shows that the opposite is more likely. Managers who communicate consistently in an authentic, honest, and candid manner are looked up to with respect and admired for their ethical conduct.

An Ethical Dilemma. Here's a communication scenario that has ethical implications. Put yourself in the project manager's shoes to practice applying the standards for ethical conduct presented earlier.

Problem: The project manager for a consulting assignment wonders whether some facts should be left out of a report to the sponsor because the marketing executives paying for the report would look bad if the facts were included. What is the project manager's ethical responsibility?

Solution: The PMI Standards for Ethical and Professional Conduct call for honesty and respect. Therefore, the project manager in this scenario recognizes that all facts must be reported. The project manager might also consider briefing all of the relevant managers—particularly the marketing executives—of the main findings of the report before it is officially filed. The focus, however, should be on what the sponsor cares about so that the reader can see how the information in the report can benefit the sponsor's organization. It's up to the writer to tell the story that the reader needs to hear and to advocate organizational changes based on the information.

> It's up to the writer to tell the story that the reader needs to hear.

Cultural Differences and Ethics

Because no universal laws exist, the definition of ethical behavior varies from culture to culture. One example is the taking of bribes. While illegal as well as unethical in one country, bribes are an accepted way of doing business in another. When communicating in our competitive global environment, project managers will sometimes encounter situations that test their integrity. They should be aware that cultural values will often determine communication behavior regarding directness, honesty, and completeness. Most of all, they should be guided by their profession's code of ethical conduct.

Summary

This chapter provides a look into the future. In order to ensure success, project managers should tune in to major trends in the global work environment. Four of these trends this chapter identifies and discusses are

(1) growing reliance on distributed team collaboration, (2) increasing reliance on technology, (3) expanding cultural sensitivity, and (4) heightened emphasis on ethics.

The first trend, growing reliance on collaboration across boundaries, calls for project managers to use a range of tools and techniques to communicate, thereby building community, even in the presence of geographic dispersion.

The justification for our increasing reliance on technology is increased efficiency and productivity, but technology has both advantages and disadvantages. When messages are sensitive, negative, non-routine, and/or complex, face-to-face interactions may be preferable to technology. Messages generated and received at work should not be considered private or protected, as surveillance of teams' use of technology will continue to grow.

A third trend, expanding gender, age, education, and cultural diversity in the workplace, requires that managers improve their own sensitivity by becoming familiar with others' practices, principles, language, and preferences. Similarly, managers should help their team members develop diversity awareness through formal training, zero-tolerance for disrespect, openly discussing differences, and promoting the benefits of diversity.

The trend toward heightened emphasis on ethics requires that managers create or adopt a code of conduct and broadcast it to their teams and other stakeholders. Managers face ethical dilemmas and temptations every day, and the only way to maintain trust and integrity is to consistently follow an established code of behavior.

Questions

1. Think of a time you led or were a member of a distributed project team. What were some of the communication challenges you experienced? How were they addressed? How effective were these measures that were taken? What could have been done differently?

2. Choose a communication technology that you are familiar with and analyze its advantages and disadvantages. Choose an emerging technology that you would like to become familiar with and analyze its advantages and disadvantages.

3. Use one of the two self-assessment tools presented in the section on developing culturally sensitive project teams. Think about the results and form a plan of action for improvement.

4. Compose a code of conduct for ethical behavior in your profession.

Notes

Chapter 1

1. Ahsan, Ho, and Khan (2013, pp. 36–54).
2. Buelt and Plowman (2018, pp. 83–141).
3. Jones (2014).
4. Towers Watson, Inc. (2013).
5. Project Management Institute Inc. (2013).
6. PMBOK® Guide (2017, pp. 361–62).
7. PMBOK® Guide (2017, Table X6-1).
8. PMBOK® Guide (2017, pp. 19–20).
9. Phillips (2015).
10. McWorthy and Henningsen (2014, pp. 123–37).
11. Hargie, Tourish, and Wilson (2001, pp. 414–36).
12. Project Management Institute, Inc. (2013).
13. Schwartz and Porath (2014).
14. Lohr (2014).
15. Grant (2013).
16. Grant (2013, p. 265).

Chapter 2

1. PMBOK® Guide (2017, pp. 548–666).
2. Wells and Kloppenborg (2019, pp. 4–9).
3. Hoogveld (2018, pp. 79–86).
4. Ross (2014. p. D3).
5. Towers Watson, Inc. (2013).
6. Morris and Leung (2000, pp. 100–132).
7. Rosenberg (2018, p. B4).
8. "Leadership in Diversity and Inclusion" (2014, p. 56).
9. Kochan, et al. (2003, pp. 3–21).
10. Jayne and Dipboye (2004, pp. 409–424).
11. Sarnoff (2014, p. D1).
12. Tannen (1990).
13. Wood (2013).
14. Grant and Sandberg (2014, p. 3SR).
15. Hart Research Associates (2013).

16. Bolchover (2012, p. 11).
17. Gladwell (2008, p. 175).
18. Hofstede (1980, pp. 42–63).
19. Gudykunst (2004).
20. Kameda (2014, p. 102).

Chapter 3

1. Munter (2012, p. 154).
2. Wood (2013, p. 127).
3. Williams (2018, p. 48).
4. Grant (2013, p. 265).
5. Huang et al. (2017, pp. 430–452).
6. Garner (2011, pp. 3–16).
7. Hamilton (2013).
8. Kolb and Fry (1975).
9. Kirkpatrick and Kirkpatrick (2007).
10. Becker and Klimoski (1989).
11. Cederblom (1992, pp. 310–321).
12. Erbert (2014, pp. 138–158).
13. Putnam and Wilson (1988).
14. Hoffman, Harburg and Meier (1962, pp. 206–224).
15. Donohue, Diez and Stahl (1983, pp. 249–279).

Chapter 4

1. Bryant (2014, p. 2).
2. McGregor (1960).
3. Edelman Trust Barometer (2012).
4. Sigmar, Hynes, and Hill (2012, pp. 301–317).
5. Ryback (2012).
6. Goleman (1995).
7. Vickery (1984, pp. 59–64).
8. Wells and Kloppenborg (2019, p. 42).
9. Schwartz and Porath (2014).
10. Carroll (2006).
11. Grant (2013, pp. 58–59.)
12. Mishra, Boynton, and Mishra (2014, p. 191).
13. Sower, Duffy, and Kohers (2008).
14. Wells and Kloppenborg (2019, p. 47).
15. Anantatmula (2016, pp. 59–60).

Chapter 5

1. Anantatmula (2016, p. 107).
2. Towers Watson, Inc. (2013).
3. Hughes (2004, p. 10).
4. Hynes and Veltsos (2019).
5. PMBOK® Guide (2017).
6. Radicati Group (2014).
7. Murray (2018).
8. Russ, Daft, and Lengel (1990, pp. 151–75).
9. Wen, Schwieger, and Gershuny (2007).
10. Elmuti and Davis (2006).
11. Guerin (n.d).
12. American Management Association (2014).
13. Towers Watson, Inc. (2013).
14. Sotomayor (2014, p. 199).
15. Bennett (1986, pp. 179–96).
16. Bolchover (2012, p. 11).
17. Towers Watson, Inc. (2013).
18. Project Management Institute, Inc. (2013).
19. Rasberry (2013).
20. Wells and Kloppenborg (2019).

References

Ahsan, K., M. Ho, and S. Khan. 2013. "Recruiting Project Managers: A Comparative Analysis of Competencies and Recruitment Signals from Job Ads." *Project Management Journal* 44, no. 5, pp. 36–54.

American Management Association. June 2, 2014. "The Latest on Employee Surveillance." Retrieved from http://amanet.org/training/articles/The-Latest-on-Workplace-Monitoring-and-Surveillance.aspx

Anantatmula, V.S. 2016. *Project Teams: A Structured Development Approach*. New York, NY: Business Expert Press.

Becker, B.E., and R.J. Klimoski. 1989. "A Field Study of the Relationship between the Organizational Feedback Environment and Performance." *Personnel Psychology* 42, no. 3, pp. 343–58.

Bennett, M.J. 1986. "A Developmental Approach to Training for Intercultural Sensitivity." *International Journal of Intercultural Relations* 10, no. 2, pp. 179–96.

Bolchover, D. 2012. "Competing Across Borders: How Cultural and Communication Barriers Affect Business." *The Economist Intelligence Unit Ltd. Report*, p. 11.

Bryant, A.L. August 3, 2014. "See Yourself as Others See You: Interview with Sharon Sloane." *The New York Times*, p. 2.

Buelt, M., and C. Plowman. 2018. *Developing Strengths Based Project Teams*. New York, NY: Business Expert Press.

Carroll, A.B. July 29, 2006. "Trust is the Key When Rating Great Workplaces." Retrieved from http://onlineathens.com/stories/073006/business_20060730047.shtml

Cederblom, D. 1992. "The Performance Appraisal Interview: A Review, Implications, and Suggestions." In *Readings in Organizational Communication*, ed. K.L. Hutchinson. Dubuque, IA: Wm. C. Brown.

Donohue, W.A., M.E. Diez, and R.B. Stahl. 1983. "New Directions in Negotiations Research." In *Communication Yearbook* 7, ed. R.N. Bostrom. Beverly Hills, CA: Sage Publications.

Edelman Trust Barometer. 2012. *Executive Summary*. Retrieved from http://scribd.com/doc/79026497/2012-Edelman-Trust-Barometer-Executive-Summary

Elmuti, D., and H.H. Davis. 2006. "Not Worth the Bad Will." *Industrial Management* 48, no. 6, pp. 26–30.

Erbert, L.A. 2014. "Antagonistic and Non-Antagonistic Dialectical Contradictions in Organizational Conflict." *International Journal of Business Communication* 51, no. 2, pp. 138–58.

Garner, J.L. 2011. "How Award-winning Professors in Higher Education Use Merrill's First Principles of Instruction." *International Journal of Instructional Technology and Distance Learning* 8, no. 5, pp. 3–16. See also: Merrill, M.D. 2002. "First Principles of Instruction." *Educational Technology Research and Development* 50, no. 3, pp. 43–59.

Gladwell, M. 2008. *Outliers: The Story of Success*. New York, NY: Little, Brown and Company.

Goleman, D. 1995. *Emotional Intelligence*. New York, NY: Bantam Publishing Co.

Grant, A.M. 2013. *Give and Take: A Revolutionary Approach to Success*. New York, NY: Viking Press.

Grant, A., and S. Sandberg. December 7, 2014. "Women at Work: When Talking about Bias Backfires." *The New York Times*, p. 3SR.

Gudykunst, W.B. 2004. *Bridging Differences: Effective Intergroup Communication*, 4th ed. Thousand Oaks, CA: Sage.

Guerin, L. n.d. "Monitoring Employee Communications: Learn the Rules on Monitoring Email, Voicemail, Telephone Conversations, and Internet Use." Retrieved from http://nolo.com/legal-encyclopedia/monitoring-employee-communications-29853.html

Hamilton, C. 2013. *Communicating for Results: A Guide for Business and the Professions*, 10th ed. Boston, MA: Cengage.

Hargie, O., D. Tourish, and N. Wilson. 2001. "Communication Audits and the Effects of Increased Information: A Follow-Up Study." *Journal of Business Communication* 39, no. 4, pp. 414–36. See also Thomas, G.F., R. Zolin, and J.L. Hartman. 2009. "The Central Role of Communication in Developing Trust and Its Effect on Employee Involvement." *Journal of Business Communication* 46, no. 3, pp. 287–310.

Hart Research Associates. 2013. *It Takes More than a Major: Employer Priorities for College Learning and Student Success*. Washington, DC: Association of American Colleges and Universities.

Hoffman, L.R., E. Harburg, and N.R. Meier. 1962. "Differences and Disagreements as Factors in Creative Problem-Solving." *Journal of Abnormal and Social Psychology* 64, no. 2, pp. 206–24.

Hofstede, G. 1980, Summer. "Motivation, Leadership and Organization: Do American Theories Apply Abroad?" *Organizational Dynamics* 9, no. 1, pp. 42–63.

Hoogveld, M. 2018. *Agile Management: The Fast and Flexible Approach to Continuous Improvement and Innovation in Organizations*. New York, NY: Business Expert Press.

Huang, K., M. Yeomans, A.W. Brooks, J. Minson, and F. Gino. 2017. "It Doesn't Hurt to Ask: Question-Asking Increases Liking." *Journal of Personality and Social Psychology* 113, no. 3, pp. 430–52.

Hughes, L. January-February, 2004. "Do's and Don'ts of Effective Team Leadership." *WIB, Magazine of the American Business Women's Association.*

Hynes, G.E., and J.R. Veltsos. 2019. *Managerial Communication: Strategies and Applications*, 7th ed. Thousand Oaks, CA: SAGE Publications, Inc.

Jayne, M.E., and R.L. Dipboye. 2004. "Leveraging Diversity to Improve Business Performance: Research Findings and Recommendations for Organizations." *Human Resource Management* 43, no. 4, pp. 409–24.

Jones, J. February 25, 2014. "Communication Skills Most Needed by Individual Contributors." *American Management Association.* Retrieved from http://amanet.org/news/9791.aspx

Kameda, N. 2014. "Japanese Business Discourse of Oneness: A Personal Perspective." *International Journal of Business Communication* 51, no. 1, pp. 93–113.

Kirkpatrick, D.L., and J.D. Kirkpatrick. 2007. *Implementing the Four Levels.* Oakland, CA: Berrett-Koehler Publishers.

Kochan, T., K. Bezrukova, R. Ely, S. Jackson, A. Joshi, K. Jehn, J. Leonard, D. Levine, and D. Thomas. 2003. "The Effects of Diversity on Business Performance: Report of the Diversity Research Network." *Human Resource Management* 42, no. 1, pp. 3–21.

Kolb, D., and R. Fry. 1975. "Toward an Applied Theory of Experiential Learning." In *Theories of Group Process*, ed. C. Cooper. London, UK: John Wiley. See also http://learningfromexperience.com

"Leadership in Diversity and Inclusion." November 9, 2014. *The New York Times Magazine*, pp. 54–58.

Lohr, S. June 21, 2014. "Unblinking Eyes Track Employees: Workplace Surveillance Sees Good and Bad." *The New York Times.* Retrieved from http://nytimes.com/2014/06/22/technology/workplace-surveillance-sees-good-and-bad.html?_r=0

McGregor, D. 1960. *The Human Side of Enterprise.* New York, NY: McGraw-Hill.

McWorthy, L., and D.D. Henningsen. 2014. "Looking at Favorable and Unfavorable Superior-Subordinate Relationships through Dominance and Affiliation Lenses." *International Journal of Business Communication* 51, no. 2, pp. 123–37.

Mishra, K., L. Boynton, and A. Mishra. 2014. "Driving Employee Engagement: The Expanded Role of Internal Communications." *International Journal of Business Communication* 51, no. 2, p. 183–202.

Morris, M., and K. Leung. 2000. "Justice for All? Progress in Research on Cultural Variation in the Psychology of Distributive and Procedural Justice." *Applied Psychology: An International Review* 49, no. 1, pp. 100–32.

Munter, M. 2012. *Guide to Managerial Communication: Effective Business Writing and Speaking*, 9th ed. Upper Saddle River, NJ: Prentice Hall.

Murray, M. June 15, 2018. "Blockchain Explained." *A Reuters Visual Guide.* Retrieved from http://graphics.reuters.com/TECHNOLOGY-BLOCKCHAIN/010070P11GN/index.html

Phillips, J.H. 2015. "Real World Project Management: Communications." Retrieved from http://projectsmart.co.uk/real-world-project-management-communications.php

PMBOK® Guide. 2017. *A Guide to the Project Management Body of Knowledge*, 6th ed. Newtown Square, PA: Project Management Institute.

Project Management Institute, Inc. 2013. *The High Cost of Low Performance: The Essential Role of Communications.* Pulse of the Profession In-depth Report. Retrieved from www.pmi.org

Putnam, L.L., and S.R. Wilson. 1988. "Argumentation and Bargaining Strategies as Discriminators of Integrative and Distributive Outcomes." In *Managing Conflict: An Interdisciplinary Approach*, ed. A. Rahim. New York, NY: Praeger Publishers.

Radicati Group. 2014. "Email Statistics Report, 2013-2017." Retrieved from http://radicati.com/wp/wp_content/uploads/2013/04/Email-Statistics-Report-2013-2017-Executive -Summary.pdf

Rasberry, R. March 15, 2013. "A Study of How Fortune 100 Companies Communicate Ethics, Governance, Corporate Responsibility, Sustainability, and Human Rights." Paper presented at the Association for Business Communication-Southwestern U.S. Annual Conference, Albuquerque, NM.

Rosenberg, J.M. December 30, 2018. "Companies Transform Cultures as They Compete for Staffers." *Houston Chronicle*, p. B4.

Ross, J. August 3, 2014. "An Appeal to Our Inner Judge." *The New York Times*, p. D3.

Russ, G.S., R.L. Daft, and R.H. Lengel. 1990. "Media Selection and Managerial Characteristics in Organizational Communications." *Management Communication Quarterly* 4, no. 2, pp. 151–75.

Ryback, D. 2012. *Putting Emotional Intelligence to Work.* New York, NY: Routledge.

Sarnoff, N. June 13, 2014. "Younger Workers Crave 'Sense of Place' on the Job." *Houston Chronicle*, p. D1.

Schwartz, T., and C. Porath. June 1, 2014. "Why You Hate Work." *The New York Times.* p. 1.

Sigmar, L.S., G.E. Hynes, and K.L. Hill. 2012. "Strategies for Teaching Social and Emotional Intelligence in Business Communication." *Business Communication Quarterly* 75, no. 3, pp. 301–17.

Sotomayor, S. 2014. *My Beloved World.* New York, NY: Vintage Books.

Sower, V.E., J.A. Duffy, and G. Kohers. 2008. *Benchmarking for Hospitals: Achieving Best-in-Class Performance without Having to Reinvent the Wheel.* Milwaukee, WI: American Society for Quality.

Tannen, D. 1990. *You Just Don't Understand: Women and Men in Conversation,* 42. New York, NY: William Morrow.

Towers Watson, Inc. 2013. *Change and Communication ROI Study—The 10th Anniversary Report.* Retrieved from www.towerswatson.com

Vickery, H.B. January, 1984. "Tapping into the Employee Grapevine." *Association Management* 36, no. 1, pp. 59–63.

Wells, K.N., and T.J. Kloppenborg. 2019. *Project Management Essentials,* 2nd ed. New York, NY: Business Expert Press.

Wen, H.J., D. Schwieger, and P. Gershuny. 2007. "Internet Usage Monitoring in the Workplace: Its Legal Challenges and Implementation Strategies." *Information Systems Management* 24, no. 2, pp. 185–96.

Williams, G.C. December, 2018. "Lend Me Your Ear: The Secret to Business Success? Listening." *Hemispheres.* United Airlines Magazine.

Wood, J.T. 2013. *Gendered Lives: Communication, Gender, and Culture,* 10th ed. Boston: Wadsworth.

About the Author

Geraldine E. Hynes, PhD, is an award-winning, internationally experienced professional communication specialist. She offers consulting, coaching, and customized training services in team communication, presentation skills, business writing, interpersonal relations, management communication, and organizational communication.

She is a retired Professor from the College of Business Administration, Sam Houston State University, Huntsville, Texas, USA, where she taught undergraduate and graduate courses both on campus and online.

Dr. Hynes is the author or coauthor of four book chapters, 41 refereed journal articles, three invited articles, and seven books. Her major books are:

- *Managerial Communication: Strategies and Applications,* 7th edition (SAGE, 2019)
- *Get Along, Get It Done, Get Ahead: Interpersonal Communication in the Diverse Workplace* (Business Expert Press, 2015)

Dr. Hynes is a Past President of the Association for Business Communication. She also served on the Board of Directors of the Association of Professional Communication Consultants and currently consults for the Center for Plain Language.

Index

OTHER TITLES IN OUR PORTFOLIO AND PROJECT MANAGEMENT COLLECTION

Timothy J. Kloppenborg, Editor

- *Attributes of Project-Friendly Enterprises* by Vittal S. Anantatmula and Parviz F. Rad
- *Stakeholder-led Project Management: Changing the Way We Manage Projects* by Louise M. Worsley
- *Innovative Business Projects: Breaking Complexities, Building Performance, Volume One: Fundamentals and Project Environment* by Rajagopal
- *Innovative Business Projects: Breaking Complexities, Building Performance, Volume Two: Financials, New Insights, and Project Sustainability* by Rajagopal
- *Why Projects Fail: Nine Laws for Success* by Tony Martyr
- *Project-Based Learning: How to Approach, Report, Present, and Learn from Course-Long Projects* by Harm-Jan Steenhuis and Lawrence Rowland
- *Adaptive Project Planning* by Louise Worsley and Christopher Worsley
- *The Lost Art of Planning Projects* by Louise Worsley and Christopher Worsley

Announcing the Business Expert Press Digital Library

Concise e-books business students need for classroom and research

This book can also be purchased in an e-book collection by your library as

- a one-time purchase,
- that is owned forever,
- allows for simultaneous readers,
- has no restrictions on printing, and
- can be downloaded as PDFs from within the library community.

Our digital library collections are a great solution to beat the rising cost of textbooks. E-books can be loaded into their course management systems or onto students' e-book readers. The **Business Expert Press** digital libraries are very affordable, with no obligation to buy in future years. For more information, please visit **www.businessexpertpress.com/librarians**. To set up a trial in the United States, please email **sales@businessexpertpress.com**.

www.ingramcontent.com/pod-product-compliance
Lightning Source LLC
Chambersburg PA
CBHW061320220326
41599CB00026B/4966